CLYDE W. SUMMERS is Professor of Law at the University of Pennsylvania. He has done pioneer studies on union discipline of its members, and has written extensively on internal union affairs, including some of the classic articles on the duty of fair representation. Mr. Summers has been active in the work of the American Civil Liberties Union and contributed to some of the ACLU's early publications on union democracy. He is co-author of the casebook *Cases and Materials on Labor Law*. Mr. Summers was in Europe during the academic year 1977-1978, studying under a grant from the National Endowment for the Humanities.

ROBERT J. RABIN is Professor of Law at Syracuse University. He is a co-author of a recently published casebook in the series *Labor Law and Social Problems*. He has written several law review articles, including a study of fair representation in arbitration. Mr. Rabin is on the Board of Directors of the Central New York Chapter of the New York Civil Liberties Union. He was Secretary of the American Bar Association Section on Labor Law for 1978-1979.

AN AMERICAN
CIVIL LIBERTIES
UNION HANDBOOK

THE
RIGHTS OF
UNION MEMBERS

Clyde W. Summers and
Robert J. Rabin

General Editor of this series
Norman Dorsen, *Chairperson ACLU*

A DISCUS BOOK/PUBLISHED BY AVON BOOKS

THE RIGHTS OF UNION MEMBERS is an original
publication of Avon Books. This work has never
before appeared in book form.

AVON BOOKS
A division of
The Hearst Corporation
959 Eighth Avenue
New York, New York 10019

First Discus Printing, November, 1979

DISCUS TRADEMARK REG. U.S. PAT. OFF. AND IN
OTHER COUNTRIES, MARCA REGISTRADA, HECHO EN
U.S.A.

Printed in the U.S.A.

Acknowledgments

Several practitioners and scholars in the field of labor relations reviewed a final draft of this manuscript. We are indebted to Professor James B. Atleson of SUNY, Buffalo; Professor Patricia E. Eames, of Antioch School of Law; Bernard T. King, Esq., an attorney in Syracuse, New York, who represents labor unions; and Herman Benson, Director of the Association for Union Democracy, for their generous commitment of time and perceptive suggestions. In the end, however, particularly in a field in which people strongly hold different positions, the responsibility for the content and viewpoints of this book belongs to us.

We also gratefully acknowledge the invaluable research assistance of Linda Jaekh, a student at Syracuse University College of Law.

Contents

Preface

This guide sets forth your rights under present law and offers suggestions on how you can protect your rights. It is one of a continuing series of handbooks published in cooperation with the American Civil Liberties Union.

The hope surrounding these publications is that Americans informed of their rights will be encouraged to exercise them. Through their exercise, rights are given life. If they are rarely used, they may be forgotten and violations may become routine.

This guide offers no assurances that your rights will be respected. The laws may change and, in some of the subjects covered in these pages, they change quite rapidly. An effort has been made to note those parts of the law where movement is taking place but it is not always possible to predict accurately when the law *will* change.

Even if the laws remain the same, interpretations of them by courts and administrative officials often vary. In a federal system such as ours, there is a built-in problem of the differences between state and federal law, not to speak of the confusion of the differences from state to state. In addition, there are wide variations in the ways in which particular courts and administrative officials will interpret the same law at any given moment.

If you encounter what you consider to be a specific abuse of your rights you should seek legal assistance. There are a number of agencies that may help you, among them ACLU affiliate offices, but bear in mind that the ACLU is a limited-purpose organization. In many communities, there are federally funded legal service offices which provide assistance to poor persons who cannot afford the costs of legal representation. In general, the rights that the ACLU defends are freedom of inquiry and expression; due process of law; equal protection of the laws; and privacy. The authors in this series have discussed other rights in these books (even though they sometimes fall outside the ACLU's usual concern) in order to provide as much guidance as possible.

These books have been planned as guides for the people directly affected: therefore the question and answer format. In some of these areas there are more detailed works available for "experts." These guides seek to raise the largest issues and inform the non-specialist of the basic law on the subject. The authors of the books are themselves specialists who understand the need for information at "street level."

No attorney can be an expert in every part of the law. If you encounter a specific legal problem in an area discussed in one of these handbooks, show the book to your attorney. Of course, an attorney will not be able to rely *exclusively* on the handbook to provide you with adequate representation. But if she or he hasn't had a great deal of experience in the specific area, the handbook can provide helpful suggestions on how to *proceed*.

Norman Dorsen, Chairperson
American Civil Liberties Union

The principle purpose of this handbook, and others in this series, is to inform individuals of their legal rights. The authors from time to time suggest what the law should be, but the author's personal views are not necessarily those of the ACLU. For the ACLU's position on the issues discussed in this handbook, the reader should write to Librarian, ACLU, 22 East 40th Street, New York, N.Y. 10016.

Introduction

For nearly thirty million workers employed under collective agreements, the union that represents them in collective bargaining is often the most important organization in their work lives. The union, in bargaining with the employer, is the individual worker's sole spokesman, and the contract the union signs is binding on the individual.

The collective agreement negotiated by the union governs who shall work and who shall not work by its apprenticeship rules, its seniority clauses, and its retirement provisions. It prescribes for the individual worker her wage rates, hours of work, holidays and vacations; it regulates her job promotions, work assignments and plant conduct; and it may provide her benefits from maternity leave to dental care and funeral costs.

The individual worker is not only governed by an industrial code negotiated by the union with the employer, but he looks to the union to enforce his rights under that code. If an individual believes he has been wrongfully laid off, underpaid, denied a promotion or unjustly discharged, his grievance is filed with the union steward, processed by the union committee, and carried to arbitration by the union.

The fact that the union benefits and protects all those it represents—whether they are members or not —does not decrease the importance to the individual of his rights as a member of the union and his participation in helping make its decisions. The collective agreement provides employees with benefits they would not otherwise enjoy, but the amount and allocation of those benefits is negotiated by the union. The collective agreement creates rights in individual employees, but those rights are defined in the union's negotiations and enforced through the union's grievance procedure. The collective agreement protects employees against arbitrary action to which they would otherwise be vulnerable, but protection is realized by the union's processing a grievance. Indeed, the fact that the union, as representative of the employees, undertakes to act on their behalf, and is expected by them to act on their behalf, is the primary source for defining the member's rights in the union and in its decision-making process.

Although the analogy is imperfect, collective bargaining is a system of industrial legislation. The collective agreement embodies rules that govern the individual's working life. The grievance procedure creates an administrative structure that interprets and enforces this body of industrial law. The union, as representative of the employees, is a basic element of that industrial government, and its power over individual workers has some of the qualities of governmental power. The rights of individual workers with reference to the union are much like the rights of citizens with reference to their government.

The law, in defining the rights of union members within their union, has built substantially on this analogy. For example, in the Labor Management Reporting and Disclosure Act of 1959 (LMRDA), commonly known as the Landrum-Griffin Act, Title I is entitled Bill of Rights of Members of Labor Organizations. Among the rights protected are equal rights to nominate candidates, vote, attend meetings, and participate in union decisions, rights of freedom of speech and assembly, and right to a fair trial; and Title IV requires that union officers be elected by secret ballot and prescribes a web of rules to insure free and fair elections.

In addition to these rights of union members to democratic processes in their unions, all workers covered by a collective agreement, whether union members or not, have a right to be fairly represented by the union. In the words of the Supreme Court, the law imposes on the union "at least as exacting a duty to protect equally the interests of the members of the craft as the Constitution imposes on a legislature to give equal protection to the interests of those for whom it legislates."

Beyond these rights to democratic processes within the union, and the right to fair and equal treatment by the union, individual workers have certain general rights of freedom of association, freedom to choose which political causes they will support, and freedom to engage or not to engage in union action. These rights might be roughly described as the right not to belong to the union and not to support its objectives.

All of these rights are encompassed within the scope of this book. Obviously, the questions cannot be complete, nor can the answers be precise. The purpose is not to provide a detailed legal handbook, but to provide a general framework that will enable workers to have a better understanding and appreciation of their rights. The questions and answers are based primarily on unions bargaining in the private sector and governed by federal law. The special problems of public employees governed by state law have largely been omitted.

I

Union Powers and Workers' Rights

What is the source of the union's power over the individual worker?

The National Labor Relations Act (NLRA) and other collective-bargaining statutes provide that a union designated by the majority of employees in a bargaining unit "shall be the exclusive representative of all employees in such unit for purposes of collective bargaining." [1] By Statute, the majority union is empowered to represent *all* employees in the bargaining unit, whether they are union members or not; and the collective agreement negotiated by the majority union binds all employees, whether they agree to the contract or not. The majority union, like a legislature, legally represents and governs all employees in the bargaining unit. The collective agreement, like legislation, is equally binding on all covered by its terms.

Can an individual worker or group of workers negotiate directly with the employer for themselves to obtain better terms or different terms than those in the collective agreement?

No, unless the majority union consents. Once a majority union has been designated, the individual loses his freedom of contract; for the majority union is the *exclusive* representative, and the employer is legally barred from negotiating with anyone else. An individual cannot be paid higher wages or be given better terms than those provided by the collective agreement, for in the words of the Supreme Court,

> The practice and philosophy of collective bargaining looks with suspicion on such individual advantages. . . . The workman is free, if he values his own bargaining position more than that of the group, to vote against representation; but the majority rules, and if it collectivizes the employment bargain, individual advantages or favors will generally in practice go in as a contribution to the collective result.[2]

Similarly, the individual cannot agree to accept lower wages or lesser benefits than those provided by the collective agreement. Any such individual agreement is invalid, and the individual can sue for full payment; also the employer is liable for breach of the collective agreement and is guilty of an unfair labor practice for making such an individual agreement.[3]

Some collective agreements prescribe only minimum wages or other benefits, leaving individuals free to bargain for terms above the minimum. Such agreements are unusual, except in the performing arts.

Although barred from negotiating contractual terms, individuals may, so far as the statute is concerned, present grievances to their employer; and the employer may adjust those grievances as long as the adjustment is not inconsistent with the terms of the collective agreement and the union has been given opportunity to be present at the adjustment.[4] In practice, however, most collective agreements give the union exclusive control over processing grievances beyond the first step and carrying grievances to arbitration.

How is the majority union designated or selected?

The union may obtain, from a majority of the employees in an appropriate bargaining unit, signed membership cards or cards authorizing it to act as bargaining representatives. On the basis of these cards the employer may grant the union recognition as exclusive representative. Otherwise, the union may petition the National Labor Relations Board (NLRB) for an election by showing membership or authorization cards signed by 30 percent of the employees in the bargaining unit. In that election, which is by secret ballot, any union that makes a substantial showing of support (generally 10 percent) may have its name included on the ballot. The choice of "No Union" is also included on the ballot. If no choice obtains a majority of all votes cast, a runoff election is held between the two highest choices. A union that receives a majority, either in the initial voting or the runoff, is certified by the NLRB as the bargaining representative. If the choice "No Union" receives a majority, then there is no exclusive representative, but each union can legally bargain for its members only. In practice, however, this seldom occurs; if the vote is for "No Union," there is normally no collective bargaining.

A new election cannot be held for a period of one year, and if the majority union negotiates an agreement, an election will not be held until the expiration of the agreement or three years after the agreement is made, if the agreement is for a longer term.[5]

Does an individual who is working under a collective agreement automatically become a member of the majority union?

No. Certification by the NLRB or recognition by the employer of a majority union does not itself change in any way the union membership status of any employee. The majority union becomes the exclusive representative of all employees, but individual employees may be members of another union, or of no union at all.

Can a worker be required to become a member of the majority union and maintain good standing in that union?

The majority union, by negotiating a "union shop" or "agency shop" agreement, can require all employees to tender regular dues and initiation fees as a condition of employment. However, the union cannot require an employee to become a "full member," pay special assessments, attend union meetings, or obey union rules as a condition of employment. Questions concerning the rights of individuals under union security agreements are developed in Chapter VIII.

What is the obligation of the union toward an individual worker who is not a member of the union?

The majority union, as the exclusive representative, has a duty to represent all employees, "the majority as well as the minority, and it is to act for and not against those whom it represents." The union, in "the exercise of its granted power to act in behalf of the others," assumes "the duty to exercise the power in their interest and behalf." The statute requires the union "to represent non-union and minority union members . . . without hostile discrimination, fairly, impartially, and in good faith." [6] The union's duty of fair representation, both in negotiating agreements and in handling grievances, will be dealt with in Chapter VII.

Why should an individual worker join a union when he is not required to do so?

First and foremost, because he or she believes in unions and collective bargaining as essential to a just and democratic industrial society. Only through unions can workers bargain effectively with employers to obtain better wages and benefits, protect themselves from arbitrary treatment, and establish a system of law and justice in the workplace. Only through collective action can a worker have a voice in fixing the terms under which he works and introduce an element of democracy into the government of industry.

Second, he should join because the union as majority representative is bargaining on his behalf, obtaining benefits in which he shares, providing protection he enjoys, and processing his grievances to secure in full measure those benefits and protection. As a beneficiary of the union's efforts, the individual has a sense of responsibility to join with fellow employees in supporting the union.

A third reason for joining is that he wants to have a voice in the decisions of the union and the choice of its leadership. The majority union, in negotiating agreements and processing grievances, vitally affects every significant aspect of his working life. Only by being a member of the union can he help shape negotiating policies, vote on proposed agreements, discuss pending grievances, or vote on the officers who speak and act for the union. The employee joins the union because he wants to become a full citizen in his branch of industrial government, participating in its decisions and sharing its responsibilities.

What is the importance of the union constitution?

The union constitution is the basic law governing the operation of the union and defining the rights and duties of union members. It is said to be a "contract" between the members and the union and is legally binding on both the members and the union. If the constitution provides that trials of members shall be conducted by an elected trial committee, a trial by the local executive board violates the "contract" and any disciplinary penalty will be set aside by the courts. If the constitution provides that a union officer can be removed only by a vote of the local union, an attempt by the local executive board or by the international president to remove the officer will be enjoined by the courts. If the constitution provides that local union officers shall be elected every two years, a suit can be brought to compel the holding of an election as the constitution requires. If the constitution makes members subject to fines for crossing a picket line, a member can, after notice and hearing, be fined and a suit can be brought in court to collect the fine.

Union constitutions are frequently quite complex and elaborate documents, defining the powers of union officers; setting out offenses for which members may be disciplined; prescribing procedures for trials, elections, referendums, and other matters; stating the purposes for which union funds may be spent and who shall be responsible; and defining the relation between the parent or international union and its local unions. All of these provisions are a part of the "contract" creating legal rights and duties enforceable in the courts.

Can a union member know what his rights and duties within the union are merely by reading the union constitution?

Not entirely. First, many constitutional provisions

are very vague or ambiguous, and the courts are the final interpreters. The offense of "causing dissension" may be interpreted to include assaulting a business agent but to exclude organizing an opposition faction in the union. Procedural provisions may be literally read and strictly enforced, or they may be loosely read and flexibly applied. Until the court has spoken, a member can not be certain what the constitution says.

Second, the courts may declare certain constitutional provisions to be invalid because they are illegal or contrary to public policy. Even before the Landrum-Griffin Act, or LMRDA, was passed in 1959, state courts had declared that disciplinary provisions prohibiting members from suing the union could not be enforced, for "It was the absolute right of the plaintiffs to bring the suit, whether they could successfully maintain it or not, and they might not be expelled for doing so." Similarly, when union members were expelled on charges of "dual unionism" and "holding unauthorized meetings" for organizing an opposition group within the union to criticize union policies, the court declared, "traditionally democratic means of improving their union may be freely availed of by members without fear of harm or penalty. . . . The price of free expression and political opposition within the union cannot be at the risk of expulsion or other disciplinary action." [7] Other provisions denying members fair trials, denying members the right to vote, arbitrarily denying members the right to run for union office, or unreasonably subjecting local unions to parent control have also been invalidated. By invalidating such constitutional provisions, the courts have in fact created affirmative rights for union members to free speech, fair trial, free access to the courts, the right to vote, and the right to run for union office.

Third, the LMRDA regulates various aspects of

union government, creating and protecting a range of important rights of union members within their union. These rights are federally protected regardless of what is in the union constitution. The LMRDA and the court decisions interpreting it are now the most important source of legal rights of union members.

The union constitution is still significant. Matters not regulated by the statute are still governed by the constitution, and rights provided by the constitution are still legally enforceable. But if a provision in the union constitution conflicts with the statute, or if the constitution fails to protect or encroaches on a right protected by the statute, then the statute, not the constitution, is the law.

What areas of union government are regulated by the LMRDA?

The act has five substantive titles, each focusing on particular union processes or membership rights.

Title I, aptly headed Bill of Rights of Members of Labor Organizations, guarantees to every member five categories of rights:

1. Equal rights and privileges to nominate candidates, to vote in elections and referendums, to attend membership meetings, and to participate in the deliberation and voting in such meetings.

2. The right to meet and assemble freely with other members; to express any views, arguments, and opinions; and to express at union meeting any views upon candidates or upon any business before the meeting.

3. The right to vote by secret ballot on any increase of union dues or assessments by the local union; and the right either to a referendum vote, or to a majority vote of delegates at a convention, on any increase at a district or national union level.

4. The right to sue or initiate administrative proceedings, whether against the union and its officers or not; the right to appear as a witness in any proceedings; and the right to petition or communicate with any legislator.

5. The right not to be disciplined unless served with specific charges and afforded a full and fair hearing.

Title II requires unions and union officers to file with the Secretary of Labor various organizational and financial reports. Members must be provided with this information and have the right to examine any books, records, and accounts necessary to verify the reports.

Title III limits the power of national unions to place a local union under trusteeship, thereby exercising supervision and control over the local union and suspending its autonomy and rights of self-government.

Title IV regulates the election of union officers, from the nomination process, through the election campaign, to the counting and preserving of the ballots. The right to be a candidate, the right to distribute campaign literature, the right to support a candidate, the right to notice of the election, the right to a secret ballot and many other rights necessary to a fair and open election are protected.

Title V declares that union officers occupy positions of trust with relation to the union and imposes on them fiduciary responsibilities in handling union funds and conducting union affairs.

The five titles overlap and interlock. Denial of the right to vote, or reprisals for supporting a candidate, violate both Title I and Title IV. Spending union money to support a candidate would violate Title IV and Title V. Misreporting of the purposes for which union funds were used would violate Title II and Title

V. (See Appendix A for some of the text of the LMRDA.)

Does the LMRDA apply to all unions?

Almost. The only unions of consequence not covered are public-employee unions, and even many of them are covered. If a local union of the American Federation of Teachers represents teachers in a private school for purposes of collective bargaining, that local is governed by the LMRDA. Because the local is under the LMRDA, its parent union, the AFT, would also be covered. However, locals representing teachers in public schools would not be covered. If the national AFT should, in its own name, rather than in the name of a local, represent teachers in a private school, then the national AFT and all of its locals would be covered.[8]

Unions not covered by the LMRDA are still subject to control by state courts interpreting and enforcing union constitutions, just as other unions were prior to the passage of the act.

Why should the federal government regulate the internal process of unions rather than leave it to state courts?

Although some state courts gave substantial protection to rights of members within unions under the guise of interpreting the union constitution or declaring selective provisions invalid, that protection was erratic and incomplete. Many courts viewed unions as social clubs or fraternal orders and were reluctant to intervene in internal union affairs. Congress concluded that the state courts would not meet the need.

More compelling, Congress had conferred upon unions a special legal status by granting the power of exclusive representation. Federal law required employers to bargain with the majority union; federal law made the contract negotiated with that union binding on all employees in the bargaining unit; and federal law empowered the union to enforce that contract. In the words of the Senate Labor Committee, "The Government which gives unions this power has an obligation to insure that the officials who wield it are responsive to the desires of the men and women they represent." [9] The governmental grant of union power over individual workers imposed a governmental obligation to protect the rights of individual workers.

Has the LMRDA destroyed the autonomy of unions and deprived them of self-government?

No. The act requires the union to observe certain democratic principles and procedures, but leaves it free to determine its own policies. The law protects the process through which decisions are made, but does not prescribe the decision to be reached. The free-speech clause of Title I prevents the union from curbing open debate on union policies, and the equal-rights clause protects the right to vote on those policies, but the choice of policy is left to the union and its members. The election process is regulated by Title IV, but the members decide who is elected.

Moreover, the union is left largely free to determine its own governmental structure and decision-making process; the law requires only that it meet certain minimum democratic standards and observe certain basic democratic rights. The union need not submit contracts to referendum vote, but if it does, the referendum must be fair and members must have equal rights to vote. Disciplinary trial boards can be made up in many ways; the law requires only that they be unbiased and give a fair hearing. One of the guiding principles enunciated in drafting the statute was that government intervention should be kept to a minimum and only essential democratic rights be legally enforced. The union's own constitution, not the statute, continues to be controlling on most matters of union government.

Protection of the democratic process was in fact conceived as a way of avoiding greater governmental intervention in unions. In the words of the Senate Committee on Labor, "Given the maintenance of minimum democratic safeguards, and detailed information about the union, the individual members are fully competent to regulate union affairs." [10] Senator McClellan, in urging that a Bill of Rights be added to the statute, was more explicit: "If we want fewer laws—and want to need fewer laws—providing regulation in this field . . . we should give union members their inherent constitutional rights. By so doing we will be giving them the tools they can use themselves." [11]

Will the courts intervene to protect the rights of union members before the union has had an opportunity to recognize and protect those rights through its own procedures?

Generally not. Union constitutions commonly provide for appeals from decisions at one level of the union to higher levels of the union. Thus, a decision by a local union might be appealed to the executive board of the national union, and its decision, in turn, might be appealed to the conventions of the national union. Long prior to the LMRDA, the courts developed the general rule that they would not intervene in internal union disputes until all appeals within the union had been exhausted.

This court-made rule requiring exhaustion of internal appeals had three main roots. First, it reflected the traditional reluctance of judges to become entangled in the family fights of voluntary associations generally, a reluctance which carried over to internal union disputes. Second, it served to conserve judicial resources, because appeals might result in corrective action that would make the member's complaint moot, or the appeal might at least focus the issue and give the court some guidance. Third, it respected the autonomy of unions by giving them the first opportunity to correct their own mistakes and thereby continue to govern their own affairs.[12]

The LMRDA adopted this principle of requiring first resort to internal union procedures with somewhat varying provisions in almost every article. The articulated Congressional policy was to "preserve a maximum amount of independence and self-government by giving every international union the opportunity to correct" its own wrongs, and this policy was "rooted in the desire to stimulate labor organizations to take the initiative and independently to establish honest and democratic procedures."[13]

Must a member always exhaust all appeals within the union before a court will intervene?

No. Strict application of the bare rule that internal appeals must be exhausted would often result in hardship and oppression, effectively denying legal relief. Some union constitutions construct ladders of appeals with so many steps and so much time between steps that the member is exhausted before the appeals are. Appeal may also be futile, because it is to union officers who have prejudged the issue or who were even responsible for the decision that is being appealed. As a result, the courts created a number of exceptions to the general rule requiring exhaustion, some of the exceptions being so broadly stated as to nearly swallow the rule.

Congress in passing the LMRDA adopted the principle that unions should have an opportunity to correct their own mistakes, but expressly limited the time a member must pursue internal appeals. The Bill of Rights provision protecting the right to sue contains the proviso that a member may be required to exhaust reasonable hearing procedures, but not to exceed four months' time, before instituting legal or administrative procedures. The election article requires a member contesting an election to invoke available remedies for three months before filing a complaint with the Secretary of Labor. The member may be required to exhaust whatever appeals are available during these time limits, but once the statutory time period elapses, the member may ignore whatever further appeals procedures are provided by the union constitution.[14]

Even appeals within these time limits may be excused if the delay will work a hardship [15] or if the appeal will be futile.[16] Thus, when the president of the union takes reprisals against those supporting the candidate opposing him in an election, the court will intervene immediately, for an appeal after the election, even though within three months, will be too late.[17] Also, when a member who criticized the officers of the national union is expelled for "falsely impugning the motives or integrity of any member or officer," he is not required to appeal to the officers he criticized.[18] Such an appeal would obviously be futile, and he can sue without waiting the maximum time of four months specified in the statute. To the argument that the union had been deprived of the opportunity to correct its errors, the court responded, "the union is the victim of its own appellate structure." [19]

The courts may intervene even before the union holds a trial. For example, members who were running for union office claimed that they had been served with charges and were being brought to trial for the purpose of using the hearings to discredit them in the upcoming election. The court held that the candidates "would be irreparably injured by having to go through what they claim will be unfair hearings," and enjoined the union from proceeding with the trial.[20]

NOTES

1. NLRA § 9(a).
2. J. I. Case Co. v. NLRB, 321 U.S. 332 (1944).
3. Order of R.R. Telegraphers v. Railway Express Agency, 321 U.S. 342 (1944).
4. NLRA § 9(a).
5. See, generally, NLRA § 9(c), setting forth the NLRB's procedures for determining representative status. In certain cases, where an employer has seriously interfered with the conduct of an election, the employer may be ordered to bargain with a union that establishes its majority through authorization cards. See NLRB v. Gissel Packing Co., 395 U.S. 575 (1969).
6. Steele v. Louisville R.R., 323 U.S. 192 (1944).
7. Madden v. Atkins, 4 App. Div. 2d 1, 162 N.Y.S. 2d 576 (2nd Dep't 1957).
8. Council 61 v. AFSCME, 80 LRRM 2942 (D.C.N.J. 1972).
9. S. REP. No. 187, 86th Cong., 1st Sess. 20 (1959).
10. Report of the Committee on Labor and Public Welfare on Senate Bill 1555 (No. 187, 86th Cong. 1st Sess., 1959 pp. 6–8, 20).
11. 105 CONG. REC. 6471–6 (1959).
12. Detroy v. American Guild of Variety Artists, 286 F.2d 75 (2nd Cir. 1961).
13. Report on Senate Bill 155, *supra* note 10, p. 21; Detroy v. American Guild of Variety Artists, *supra* note 12 at 79.

14. Eisman v. Clothing Workers Baltimore Joint Bd., 496 F.2d 1313 (4th Cir. 1974).

15. Detroy v. American Guild of Variety Artists, *supra* note 12.

16. Clothing Workers Rank & File Comm. v. Clothing Workers Philadelphia Joint Bd., 473 F.2d 1303 (3rd Cir. 1973).

17. Cefalo v. Mine Workers Dist. 50, 311 F. Supp. 946 (D.D.C. 1970).

18. Wood v. Dennis, 489 F.2d 849 (7th Cir. 1973).

19. Nix v. Machinists Union Fulton Lodge No. 2, 452 F.2d 794 (5th Cir. 1972).

20. Washington Post Guild Majority v. Newspaper Guild Local 35, 91 LRRM 2391 (D.D.C. 1976).

II

The Right to Be a Union Member and to Be Free from Improper Discipline

The doorway to exercise of democratic rights within unions is union membership, for only members have the right to participate in the decisions of the union. Union membership is the worker's industrial citizenship. This chapter deals with the threshold right to become and remain a citizen in union government—the right to join a union and the right not to be expelled from the union or be subjected to other disciplinary penalties that qualify or jeopardize membership.

Does an individual worker have a right to join a union?

An individual has a right to join a union in two fairly limited senses: First, any state or federal law that prohibits workers from forming or joining unions is unconstitutional as a denial of the First Amendment right of freedom of assembly. Thus, statutes which prohibited public employees such as teachers, policemen or firemen from joining unions have been declared unconstitutional.[1] This constitutional right to join a union, however, does not necessarily carry with it a constitutional right to engage in collective bargaining or to strike.

Second, a private employer under federal or state labor-relations acts cannot prohibit his employees from joining a union. For example, the National Labor Relations Act (NLRA) proscribes, as an unfair labor practice, any discrimination in employment because of union membership. Labor-relations acts protect not only the right to join unions but the right to bargain collectively and to engage in strikes or "other concerted activities for mutual aid and protection." [2]

There is, however, no right to join a union in the sense that a union is compelled to admit applicants to membership. In the past, a limited number of unions have refused to admit blacks, other minorities, or women, and some have at times completely closed their membership. However, as we shall see, some of these exclusionary policies would today be invalid under state and federal laws prohibiting discrimination.

Can a union refuse to admit to membership workers whom it represents in collective bargaining?

Yes. A union is obligated to represent fairly all employees for whom it bargains, but it is not required to admit them to membership. The courts have, in this regard, declared unions to be "voluntary associations," like social clubs, which can decide who shall have the privilege of membership. The Supreme Court of California is a lonely exception. It recognized that "membership in a union means more than mere personal or social accommodation, . . . that the union functions as the medium for the exercise of industrial franchise," and ordered the union to admit all those for whom it bargained.[3]

Doesn't a union's refusal to admit a worker whom it represents contradict the underlying premises of the Landrum-Griffin Act?

Certainly. Denying a worker admission to the union denies him all rights to participate in the decision-making process. He is deprived of all voice or vote in union meetings, referendums, or election of officers, but he is irrevocably bound by the union's decisions in making and administering the collective agreement. However, Congress deliberately made the statutory rights applicable only to "members" and refused to include any right to become a member.

The explanation for this irrationality is that in 1959, many senators and congressmen supporting Landrum-Griffin did not want to establish a precedent by requiring unions to admit blacks or other minorities.

Are there any limitations upon the union's right to exclude from membership any worker the union pleases?

Yes. Title VII of the Civil Rights Act of 1964 makes it an unfair employment practice for any union to exclude from membership any individual because of race, color, religion, sex, or national origin. Many state fair-employment statutes have similar provisions. Unions, however, can still refuse to admit on other grounds, or can close their membership books and refuse to admit anyone.

Can a union, by refusing to admit a worker, prevent her from obtaining work or continuing on a job under a union security agreement?

No. A union security clause—that is, a provision in a collective bargaining agreement that states that an employee must join the union in order to obtain or keep his job—cannot be enforced against a worker unreasonably denied admission to the union. As the courts have said, a union can have a closed shop or a closed union, but not both. Thus, when the Bartenders Union attempted to compel the discharge under a union-shop contract of barmaids who had been denied admission to the union, the court ordered the union either to admit the barmaids or exempt them from the union-shop requirement.[4]

Under the NLRA and the Railway Labor Act (RLA), which governs labor relations in the railroad and airlines industries, a worker who merely tenders regular dues and initiation fees cannot be discharged under a union security agreement, regardless of whether the union admits him or not.[5]

Can an individual who is a member of one local union compel another local of the same national union to admit him to membership?

Sometimes. If the constitution of the parent union gives a right to transfer membership from one local to another, then the local union must accept and admit to full membership a member holding a transfer card. However, if the constitution gives the local union discretion to accept or reject transfers, then the local union can exercise its discretion to reject, even though the member seeking transfer is working in the jurisdiction of the local to which he seeks to transfer.[6]

Does the union have the same freedom to expel a member as it has to refuse to admit him to membership in the first place?

Definitely not. Once an individual is admitted, he acquires legally enforceable rights, often given substance by the courts' finding of a "property right" in membership. Once admitted, the individual becomes a party to a "contract" with the union, with the terms of that "contract" being determined by the union constitution. In principle, a member can be expelled only in accordance with the union constitution. He can be expelled only for conduct prohibited by the constitution and only through procedures prescribed by the constitution.

More importantly, by becoming a member of the union, an individual obtains protection under the LMRDA. Section 609 makes it unlawful for a union "to fine, suspend, expel, or otherwise discipline any of its members for exercising any rights to which he is entitled under the provisions of this Act." Also, the LMRDA Bill of Rights provides that "No member . . . may be fined, suspended, expelled or otherwise disciplined" except after a full and fair hearing, except for nonpayment of dues.

How specifically must the union constitution spell out the offenses for which a member can be expelled or otherwise disciplined?

Although union discipline is sometimes termed the union's system of criminal law, the offenses need not be spelled out with the specificity of criminal statutes. Although union constitutions often list a number of specific offenses, almost all constitutions include some vague or ambiguous offenses such as "disloyalty," "causing dissension," "conduct unbecoming a union member," or "activities detrimental to the best interests of the union." These may be used to expel members for conduct ranging from supporting a rival union or working during a strike, through assaulting an officer or misusing union funds, to taking bribes or stuffing the ballot box.

Courts will generally allow unions wide latitude in applying vaguely stated offenses, so long as the court believes that the conduct involved should be punishable by the union. But if individuals are disciplined for exercising political rights within the union or engaging in other conduct the court believes should not be punished, the court will overrule the union's interpretation and substitute its own so as to protect the member from discipline.[7] Courts may declare the union's application of its disciplinary provision contrary to public policy and void, but where a provision is extremely vague, such as a clause prohibiting "conduct unbecoming a union member," courts will generally not declare it to be void for vagueness, as they might a criminal statute.[8]

What limits does the LMRDA place on the kinds of conduct for which unions can expel or otherwise discipline members?

The LMRDA affirmatively protects the rights of union members to engage in certain kinds of conduct, particularly in Title I, Bill of Rights, and Title IV, Elections. Section 609 then makes it unlawful for the union to discipline a member for exercising any of those rights. A member who organizes an opposition group within the union is exercising the right of assembly protected by the Bill of Rights, and she cannot be disciplined by the union, even under a clause prohibiting "dissension" or any other clause. A member who brings suit against the union is also exercising a right protected by the Bill of Rights, and all discipline is barred, even if there is an explicit constitutional provision requiring members to exhaust appeals within the union before resorting to the courts. A member who campaigns on behalf of an insurgent candidate is exercising a right guaranteed by Title IV, and any discipline for that conduct is unlawful.

Apart from the specific instances just discussed, the LMRDA places no other limitations on conduct for which members can be expelled or otherwise disciplined. For example, they can be disciplined for assaulting a fellow member, disorderly conduct at a union meeting, destroying union property, embezzling union funds, working during a strike, or engaging in a wildcat strike. The courts, however, still require that any discipline be in accordance with the union's constitution.[9]

Apart from the LMRDA, the union may be prohibited from penalizing certain conduct because of public policy. Thus, a union cannot discipline members who refuse to engage in a wildcat strike or who cross an illegal picket line.

Is the union's freedom to impose other disciplinary penalties such as fines or suspension limited in the same way as expulsions?

Substantially, yes. If a member is suspended, even for a few months or a year, he loses all rights to participate in the union during that period. He cannot attend union meetings, join in debates as to union policies, run for union office, or vote in union elections. Suspension is, for the period, equivalent to expulsion, except that the member may be required to continue paying union dues while denied his union franchise.

A fine can have the same effect as expulsion, because unless the fine is paid, the member will be declared delinquent in his financial obligations and automatically be dropped from membership. Small fines of $10 or $50 might be no substantial obstacle to continued union participation, but a fine of $1,000 might be equivalent to expulsion. Indeed, a large fine may be more serious than expulsion, for the union may sue in court to collect the fine, even though the member would prefer to lose his union membership than to pay the amount of the fine.

The courts recognized that suspensions and fines

were, in principle, substantially equivalent to expulsion and gave parallel legal protection. The LMRDA, in both the right-to-fair-hearing provision of the Bill of Rights and in the protection-against-reprisal section, 609, links together "fine, suspend, expel or otherwise discipline," treating them as full equivalents.

What procedures must a union follow in expelling or otherwise disciplining a member?

First, the union must comply with the procedure prescribed in its own constitution. Unions often prescribe quite detailed procedural rules in their constitutions, and courts, using the contract theory, require the unions to follow those rules scrupulously, even though no unfairness is shown. If the constitution requires that charges be signed by the accusing member, unsigned charges will not do; or if the constitution specifies that the trial is to be held before the local union, a trial by an elected committee, the executive board, or a neutral outsider will be invalid.[10] If the union rules require a transcript of the hearing, making a tape recording instead may be a fatal defect.[11] However, a member who proceeds with the trial knowing that the constitution is not being followed may be precluded from later complaining about the defect, particularly if he is in no way prejudiced.

Second, the union must meet the minimum standard of fairness required by the Bill of Rights of the LMRDA. Before being disciplined, a member must be "(A) served with written specific charges; (B) given a reasonable time to prepare his defense; (C) afforded a full and fair hearing." [12] If any provision of the union constitution conflicts with these requirements, then the minimum standards of the statute, of course, prevail.

No offense, except nonpayment of dues, can be punished until the member has been tried and found guilty.

This rule applies even where the alleged offense is a highly-visible one and there is little or no doubt that it has been committed, for example, strike-breaking, working for less than union scale, or joining a rival union. A member cannot even be temporarily suspended pending trial for the offense.[18] However, the union can take temporary measures of a non-disciplinary nature, for example, removing a member from a meeting for disorderly conduct.[14]

The safeguards just discussed do not necessarily apply to the removal of officers from their positions.

What standards of procedural due process are imposed on the union by the Bill of Rights of the LMRDA?

1. *Right to have notice of charges.* By statute, the charges must be written and not oral, and they must be "specific," though how specific is difficult to define. Senator McClellan said they must be "specific enough to inform the accused member of the offense that he has allegedly committed," [15] and the Supreme Court has said the member must not be "misled or otherwise prejudiced in the presentation of his defense." [16]

It is not enough for the charge to quote the constitutional provision violated; it must state the factual circumstances and time and place of the violation to give the member a reasonable opportunity to prepare her defense. For example, it was not enough to charge that a union officer "on several occasions collected dues and did not turn in the money," without specifying from whom the money was collected and when. "One can not assume," said the court, "that an accused is guilty; that he has knowledge of his derelictions and, therefore, that he has no need to be informed of the factual details of his own wrongdoing." [17]

Also, guilt must be based on the offense charged. A

member is misled and prejudiced in presenting her defense if she is charged with one offense and then found guilty of a different, though closely related, offense.[18] Similarly, a member cannot be charged with wrongful conduct engaged in on one day and then tried for conduct engaged in on other dates as well.[19] The test of the notice is whether, under the circumstances, it gives the member charged full opportunity to prepare her defense.

2. *Right to time to prepare a defense.* The time necessary to prepare a defense depends on the offense and the circumstances. Preparing to defend against charges of misuse of union funds might take much longer than preparing to defend against charges of working during a strike; and the time needed to defend against charges of dual unionism would depend upon whether the conduct involved was joining another union or supporting a competing union in an NLRB representation election. The union, however, can seldom justify a rush to trial in any case if the member has any showing of a need for more time, for there is little harm to the union in most cases if the discipline is delayed until the member has sufficient time to prepare.

3. *Right to appear and present evidence.* Even prior to the LMRDA, the courts did not tolerate devices that substantially burdened this fundamental right. Ordering a member to stand trial in a distant city, or holding the hearing at a time when the accused or his witnesses could not attend, invalidated the proceedings.[20] More difficult is the question whether the accused can require the union to produce evidence in its possession or demand that the union use its disciplinary powers to require members to appear as witnesses. However, the statutory requirement of a "full and fair hearing" should give an accused member a right to all evidence available to the union.

4. *Right to know the evidence and to cross-examine witnesses.* The right to know the evidence is fundamental; otherwise, the accused member cannot present an effective defense. It is not enough that witnesses be interviewed behind closed doors and the accused then be told the evidence. The right to a fair hearing, the courts have said, includes the right to confront one's accusers, to hear the accusing evidence, and to cross-examine witnesses.[21] Star chambers, faceless witnesses, and untested evidence will not do. These same principles have barred the use of affidavits or other hearsay evidence that cannot be tested by cross-examination.

5. *Right to counsel.* Most unions permit a member on trial to have another member as counsel, but few permit the use of an outside lawyer. This reflects the union's general desire to keep problems "within the family" and the union's particular distrust of lawyers. The courts have upheld this barring of lawyers, declaring that "a union member need not necessarily be provided with the full panoply of procedural safeguards found in criminal proceedings." [22] All that a member is entitled to is a fair hearing, and that does not include legal counsel.[23] However, the accused member is entitled to be placed on a roughly equal footing with the accuser,[24] so if the prosecution is conducted by a lawyer, then the accused member is entitled to a lawyer.[25] The courts have discounted the usefulness of a lawyer in union trials on the grounds that the trial body is made up of union members who are not learned in the law—like a jury in a criminal case! [26]

6. *Right to an unbiased tribunal.* All members of the tribunal must come to the hearing with open, unprejudiced minds. The fact that one member of the tribunal indicates before the trial that he believes the member guilty will invalidate the discipline.[27] When a member was charged with disorderly conduct at a

meeting, it was improper to try him by a committee of officers and members who had been at the meeting.[28] They could not decide the case solely on evidence brought out at the hearing, which the accused could confront and rebut, but would inevitably be influenced by what they knew and concluded before the hearing. Also, when an officer against whom a member had filed charges sat on a trial committee trying that member on other charges, the court declared this "as a matter of fundamental due process . . . inherently improper." [29] The court relied upon a statement by the Supreme Court, in the context of a state licensing proceeding against a physician, that the danger of bias is too great when an adjudicator sits on a case "in which he has been the target of personal abuse or criticism from the party before him." [30]

The greatest danger of bias arises when discipline grows out of internal political conflict, and the courts have recognized the potential for prejudice in these situations. For example, during a bitter political fight in the United Mine Workers Union, the brother of the district president and the district secretary filed charges against those who had opposed the incumbent officers in the election and who were then challenging the election with the Department of Labor. The trial was to be held before the district executive board. Although the president and secretary disqualified themselves, the court found that it would be impossible for the accused to be treated impartially because the remaining members of the board were political allies of the president and secretary. Because of the potential bias, the court enjoined the union from even hearing the case. To the argument that union appeals had not been exhausted, the court responded: "Requiring plaintiffs to spend four months seeking a determination already well known to the court would not have fostered union self-government or advanced the policies of the LMRDA." [31]

The requirement of a "full and fair hearing" may reach any aspect of a disciplinary proceeding that obstructs full presentation of the evidence or warps fair judgment on the merits. Thus, it is a violation of this right for a prosecutor to sit in on the deliberations of a trial tribunal.

What remedies will courts give to a member who has been wrongfully disciplined by the union?

First, the court will order the union not to carry out, or to reverse, the penalty. If a member has been fined, the court will enjoin the union from enforcing the fine, or if the fine has already been paid, will order that it be returned. If a member has been suspended or expelled, the court will order the union to reinstate him with full membership rights.

Second, the court can award money damages, and damages may include compensation for loss of earnings because the discipline has resulted in being discharged or blacklisted with employers,[32] injuries to reputation, mental suffering, humiliation and other emotional distress.[33] In addition, punitive damages can be awarded where the discipline is "malicious and in reckless disregard for the rights of the plaintiff." [34] The total damages can be quite substantial. For example, a member of the Painters Union was awarded $9,900 for loss of wages, $42,500 for mental suffering, and $6,000 as punitive damages. Awards of more than $20,000 are not uncommon.[35] Both the union and the officers responsible for the wrongful discipline can be held liable for damages, including punitive damages. The union may thus be required to pay for the wrongful and even malicious conduct of its officers, even though the conduct was not authorized or ratified by the members.

Third, the court can order the union to pay the wrongfully disciplined member's lawyer's fees and litigation costs where the court finds that the member, in protecting his rights, benefited the union by vindicating the rights of all members.[36]

Under what circumstances may a union impose a fine on a member?

This depends, first of all, on the wording of the union constitution and bylaws. If they make clear that certain standards of conduct are required of a union member and that a member may be fined for failing to observe these standards, then the union has the right to fine a member. And, as indicated earlier, the union's constitution need not spell out the offense with the specificity that would be required in a criminal statute. Unions have imposed fines under their constitutions for such offenses as dual unionism, coming late to union meetings, and working with a nonunion employee.[37] In addition, courts have sustained fines imposed against members who refused to honor a picket line and instead reported for work and drew their regular pay.[38] In one case the Supreme Court upheld the right of the union to impose a fine on a member who exceeded stated production quotas and then drew his pay, rather than banking his excess earnings as required by union rule.[39]

However, certain conduct of union members is protected against union discipline, including fines, on grounds of public policy. For example, a union may not fine a member for failing to exhaust internal union remedies before filing an unfair-labor-practice charge.[40] Nor may a union fine a member who initiates a decertification petition in an effort to remove the union as bargaining agent, although it may expel or suspend the member for such an offense.[41]

How can a union enforce a fine imposed upon a member?

There are basically two ways. First, the union may expel the member for nonpayment of a fine. The right to expel for nonpayment of a fine is the same as the right to expel for any other offense, and depends upon whether the offense is spelled out in the union constitution and the procedures for determining the offense are fair. Expulsion of course deprives the member of the right to participate in union governance; for this reason, as indicated in a previous question, Section 609 of the LMRDA provides safeguards against this form of discipline.

Expulsion may not be a meaningful sanction in all cases for failure to pay a union fine. Since, as will be explained in Chapter VIII, an employee who is expelled from a union for failure to pay a fine cannot be discharged from his job on this account, the member may not care if he is expelled. The Supreme Court has recognized that, particularly in the case of a weak union, expulsion may not be an effective sanction; "where the union is weak, and membership therefore of little value, the union faced with futher depletion of its ranks may have no real choice except to condone the member's disobedience." [42]

Unions have therefore resorted increasingly in recent years to an alternative way of enforcing payment of union fines. They have instituted civil suits in court for collection of fines, arguing that the union member assumes a contractual obligation to pay any fine validly imposed under a union constitution. Individuals who have been fined have contended that the enforcement of a fine violates their Section 7 right to refrain from concerted activities. However, the Supreme Court has held that the enforcement of a fine through a lawsuit for its collection does not violate the NLRA:

> Integral to . . . federal labor policy has been the power in the chosen union to protect against erosion its status under that policy through reasonable discipline of members who violate rules and regulations governing membership. . . . Congress was operating within the context of the "contract theory" of the union-member relationship which widely prevailed at that time. The efficacy of a contract is precisely its legal enforceability. A lawsuit is and has been the ordinary way by which performance of private money obligations is compelled.[43]

What if the fine is unreasonably large or imposed through unfair procedures?

In a series of cases the NLRB and the courts have held that a union does not commit an unfair labor practice even if the fine is unreasonably large or the procedures followed by the union were unfair or did not comply with the union constitution.[44] As a result, fines as great as $2,000, perhaps equaling the money a member who refused to honor a picket line earned while working during a strike, do not violate the NLRA.[45] However, the NLRB and the courts have made clear that the amount of the fine and the fairness of the procedures are defenses that the member may raise when the union attempts to collect the fine in court.[46]

If the member resists the collection of a fine in court on the grounds that proper procedures were not followed, he could raise the same kind of considerations discussed earlier in this chapter on the propriety of union discipline. These would include the degree to which the offense was spelled out in the constitution, the adequacy of the notice of the offense, and other due process requirements already discussed. In the case of an unreasonably large fine, the member might argue that the union constitution did not make clear that a fine of such magnitude could be imposed, and that judicial enforcement of such a fine would be unconscionable.[47]

May an employee avoid a fine by not joining a union or by resigning his membership in the union?

The employee who does not join the union is not subject to a union fine, or to any other discipline, for that matter. This is a principal reason for an employee to exercise the right granted under Section 8(a)(3) of the NLRA not to join a union. The right not to join a union, even in the face of a union-security clause that appears to require membership as a condition of employment, is discussed in detail in Chapter VIII. However, most employees find it advantageous to join the union that represents them, so the significant question becomes whether a member may resign his membership in order to avoid having a fine imposed and a suit for its collection enforced.

The Supreme Court has stated that the union has the right to fine members regardless of their motivation in joining the union.[48] Thus, if a member joins a union in the mistaken belief that he was required to do so under a union-security agreement, the union nevertheless has the right to fine him. To avoid a fine, the member must resign his membership in the union. It is clear that he must do so before he commits the offense in question; if he is a member at the time he violates a union rule he is subject to a fine even if he resigns his membership before the union actually imposes the fine, conducts a hearing against the individual, or brings a lawsuit for its collection. For example, if a union calls a strike, the member who chooses to ignore the picket line and to report to work must resign before he crosses the picket line, or else he is subject to union discipline. The NLRB has rejected a union argument that unless the member resigns prior to the strike vote he is subject to discipline for violating the union's decision.[49] If the member wishes to rejoin the union, the union may force him to pay a fine imposed—even for postresignation conduct—before reinstating him.[50]

Many union constitutions do not provide specific procedures for resignation, for the question of resignation was not significant until the use of the fining power became prevalent. If there are no procedures limiting the right to resign, it is clear that the member may resign at any time.[51] And if he does so before committing any violation of his membership obligation, he may not be fined. But if the union constitution limits the right to resign, as many now do, the member may not be able to drop his membership at will. There is presently no definitive law on whether a union may place any limit on a member's right to resign, although the NLRB has held that a provision that limits the member's right to resign to a ten-day period preceding the end of the union's fiscal year is too narrow to permit the member to effectively sever his relationship with the union.[52]

NOTES

1. McLaughlin v. Tilendis, 398 F.2d 287 (7th Cir. 1978); Atkins v. City of Charlotte, 296 F.Supp. 1068 (W.D.N. Car. 1969); *compare* Elk Grove Firefighter's Local v. Willis, 400 F.Supp. 1097 (N.D. Ill. 1975), *aff'd.* 539 F.2d 715 (7th Cir. 1976).

2. NLRA § 7, 8(a)(3).

3. Thorman v. Theatrical Stage Employees Union, 49 Cal. 2d 629, 320 P. 2d 494 (Cal. Sup. Ct. 1958).

4. Wilson v. Hacker, 200 Misc. 124, 101 N.Y.S. 2d 461 (N.Y. Sup. Ct. 1950).

5. NLRA § 8(a)(3); RLA § 2, Eleventh. For further discussion of this point, see Chapter VIII.

6. Gavin v. Iron Workers Local 1, 90 LRRM 2789 (N.D. Ill. 1975); Lusk v. Plumbers Local 540, 84 LRRM 2262 (E.D. Va. 1972).

7. Salzhandler v. Caputo, 316 F.2d 445 (2nd Cir. 1963).

8. Mitchell v. International Ass'n of Machinists, 196 Cal. App. 2d 796, 16 Cal. Rptr. 813 (1961).

9. See Summers, Legal Limitations on Union Discipline, 64 Harv. L. Rev. 1049, 1074–1079 (1951).

10. Kiepura v. Steelworkers Local 1091, 358 F.Supp. 987 (N.D. Ill. 1973).

11. Hart v. Carpenters Local 1292, 341 F.Supp. 1266 (E.D.N.Y. 1972).

12. Smith v. Musicians Union, 80 LRRM 3063 (S.D.N.Y. 1972).

13. Caravan v. Typographical Union No. 860, 381 F.Supp 14 (E.D. PA. 1974). See LMRDA § 101(a)(5).

14. Ford v. Kammerer, 287 F.Supp. 853 (E.D. Pa. 1968).

15. See International Bhd. of Boilermakers v. Hardeman, 401 U.S. 233, 245 n. 12 (1971).

16. Ibid. at 245.

17. Gleason v. Chain Service Restaurant, 422 F.2d 342 (2d Cir. 1970).

18. Hartner v. Baltimore Jt. Bd, Clothing Workers, 339 F.Supp. 1257 (D. Md. 1972).

19. Eisman v. Clothing Workers Baltimore Joint Bd., 496 F.2d 1313 (4th Cir. 1974).

20. Hart v. Carpenters Local 1292, supra note 11.

21. Kiepura v. Steelworkers Local 1091, supra note 10.

22. Tincher v. Piasecki, 520 F.2d 851 (7th Cir. 1975).

23. Sawyers v. Grand Lodge, Machinists, 279 F.Supp. 747

(E.D. No. 1967); Winterberger v. Teamsters Local 162, 558 F.2d 923 (9th Cir. 1977).

24. Buresch v. Electrical Workers Local 24, 343 F.Supp. 183 (D.C. Md. 1971).

25. Cornelio v. Metropolitan Dist. Council, Carpenters Union, 243 F.Supp. 126 (E.D. Pa., 1965).

26. Ibid.

27. Stein v. Mutual Clerks Guild of Mass., 384 F.Supp. 444 (D.C. Mass. 1974); Falcone v. Dantinne, 420 F.2d 1157 (3rd Cir. 1969).

28. Kiepura v. Steelworkers Local 1091, supra note 10.

29. Tincher v. Piasecki, supra note 22.

30. Withrow v. Larkin 421 U.S. 35 (1975).

31. Semancik v. Mine Workers Dist. 5, 466 F.2d. 144 (3rd Cir. 1972).

32. Robins v. Schonfeld, 326 F.Supp. 525 (S.D. N.Y. 1971).

33. Talavera v. Teamsters Local 85, 351 F.Supp. 155 (N.D. Cal. 1972).

34. Sands v. Abelli, 290 F.Supp. 677 (S.D. N.Y. 1968).

35. Ryan v. Electrical Workers, 387 F.2d. 778 (7th Cir. 1967).

36. Hall v. Cole, 412 U.S. 1 (1973).

37. Minneapolis Star and Tribune Co., 109 NLRB 727 (1954). See generally Atleson, Union Fines and Picket Lines: the NLRA and Union Disciplinary Power, 17 U.C.L.A. L. REV. 681 (1970); Gould, Some Limitations upon Union Discipline under the NLRA, 1970 DUKE L.J. 1067.

38. NLRB v. Allis-Chalmers Mfg. Co., 388 U.S. 175 (1967).

39. Scofield v. NLRB, 394 U.S. 423 (1969). Compare Meat Cutters, Local 593, 99 LRRM 1123 (1978).

40. NLRB v. Industrial Union of Marine and Shipbuilding Workers, 391 U.S. 418 (1968).

41. Molders Local 125, 178 NLRB 208 (1969), enf'd. 442 F.2d 92 (7th Cir. 1971); Tawas Tube Products, Inc., 151 NLRB 46 (1965). See also American Broad-

casting Companies v. Writers Guild, 98 S.Ct. 627 (Sup. Ct. 1978).

42. NLRB v. Allis-Chalmers, *supra* note 38 at 183.
43. *Ibid.* at 181, 192.
44. NLRB v. Boeing Co., 412 U.S. 67 (1973); Machinists Local 504, 185 NLRB 365 (1970).
45. See NLRB v. Granite State Joint Bd., Textile Workers 409 U.S. 213 (1972).
46. NLRB v. Boeing Co., *supra* n. 44 at 76.
47. *See* the examples of lower court fine-enforcement cases discussed by the Supreme Court, *ibid.* at 76 n. 12.
48. NLRB v. Allis-Chalmers, *supra* note 38, at 196.
49. NLRB v. Granite State Joint Bd., *supra* note 45. *See* Note, *Union Power to Discipline Members Who Resign,* 86 HARV. L. REV. 1536 (1973).
50. Local 1255, Machinists v. NLRB, 456 F.2d 1214 (5th Cir. 1972). *See also* NLRB v. District Lodge 99, Machinists, 194 NLRB 938 (1972), *modified,* 489 F.2d 769 (1st Cir. 1974); Auto Workers, Local 1756, 100 LRRM 1208 (NCRB, 1979).
51. NLRB v. Granite State Joint Bd., *supra* note 45.
52. Booster Lodge 405, Machinists v. NLRB, 412 U.S. 84 (1973). *See* UAW Local 647, 197 NLRB 608 (1972).

III

The Right to Participate in Union Decisions: Equal Rights, Fair Political Process, Freedom of Speech

The right to participate is a bundle of political rights. It includes all of the rights to be a part of and act freely in the union's political process and to have a voice in union decisions. This chapter focuses mainly on those political rights guaranteed by the first three sections of the LMRDA Bill of Rights; the next chapter will deal with the rights to a fair and open election protected by Title IV.

Can a union create different classes of members with different voting and other membership rights?

Generally not. The first section of the LMRDA Bill of Rights guarantees equal rights to all members. Class A and Class B memberships—which keep some members in a subordinate position in attending or speaking at meetings, voting in elections, or exercising other political rights—are prohibited. Subsidiary or nonvoting locals that are controlled by other locals in which members of the subsidiary have no voice or vote are similarly prohibited.

Unions can, however, give certain categories, such as apprentices, limited membership status for a reasonable period, but if the "apprenticeship" is artificially prolonged to ten or fifteen years, it will be treated for what it is—a disguise for keeping some members in a permanent subordinate status. Some unions may achieve much the same result by another device. They may refuse to admit individuals actually working at the trade, but charge them a permit-card fee or service fee to use the union hiring hall. Because the individual is not admitted, he never acquires any membership rights; he remains a nonvoting dues-payer. The use of the hiring hall is explained further in Chapter VIII.

Maintaining two classes of members or local unions segregated on the basis of race, color, religion, sex, or national origin also violates the express prohibitions of Title VII of the Civil Rights Act of 1964, and this is true even though the two classes of segregated locals have equal status.

What particular rights are protected by the equal-rights clause of the Bill of Rights?

The equal-rights clause mentions six different rights:

1. to nominate candidates,
2. to vote in elections,
3. to vote in referendums,
4. to attend membership meetings,
5. to participate in deliberations, and
6. to participate in the voting on the business of such meetings.

One significant omission should be noted—the clause does not guarantee an equal right to be a candidate for union office.

By its wording, this clause of the Bill of Rights does

not guarantee any right except equality. It does not require unions to recognize any of these rights, but requires only that unions not give some members more rights than others. For example, a union is not required to submit collective agreements to referendum vote, but if it does, then all members have an equal right to vote. Even the equality of rights is "subject to reasonable rules and regulations" in the union's constitution.

However, many of these rights are affirmatively guaranteed elsewhere in the statute. For example, Title IV, Elections, requires that "a reasonable opportunity shall be given for the nomination of candidates" and guarantees that "every member in good standing shall have the right to vote" and shall be entitled to one vote. Also, the free-speech clause of the Bill of Rights guarantees to every member the right to express at union meetings his views on any business properly before the meeting.

Partly because of this overlap with other sections of the statute and partly because of the character of the rights protected, the courts have sometimes read the equal-rights clause as requiring more than bare parity of rights. It is not always an adequate defense under this clause that the union has deprived all members of their rights equally.

Does the LMRDA require direct democracy—that is, giving members a right to participate directly in union decisions?

No. The statute does not impose on unions a town-meeting form of government, but leaves unions free to choose a representative form of government. Decisions may be made in union meetings, by referendums, by elected or appointed officers, or by conventions, however the union constitution prescribes. Most unions use combinations of all of these methods, depending on the decisions to be made, but at the local-union level, direct democracy is the dominant mode, with most decisions debated and voted in the union meeting.

The statute does prescribe forms in two cases—election of officers and increase in union dues and assessments. Election of local union officers must be by membership vote; election of intermediate bodies, such as joint councils, must be by membership vote or by union officers elected by membership vote; and election of national union officers must be by membership vote or by a convention of delegates elected by membership vote. Union dues at the local level can be increased only by a local membership vote, either at a local meeting or in a referendum; union dues at other levels may be increased only by a referendum vote, or by a delegate convention, except that the executive board may increase dues pending the next regular convention.

Decisions must, of course, be made in the manner authorized by the union constitution, but apart from elections and dues increases, the union can write into its constitution any combination of direct and representative democracy. And the statute leaves the union free to decide how it shall rewrite its constitution, for the statute prescribes no procedure for amending union constitutions.

Does the principle of "one man, one vote" apply in voting dues increases?

No. When dues are increased by convention vote, all the statute requires is "a majority vote of the delegates voting," [1] and the union can decide the weighting of delegates' votes. Indeed, it is customary that the number of delegate votes of each local is not directly proportional to membership in the local, so that the larger unions are often underrepresented. [2] Such weighting does not violate either the dues-increase clause or the equal-rights clause of the Bill of Rights. All that is required is that the votes be weighted in accordance with the union constitution, and that they be accurately counted.[8]

What political rights are protected in a direct vote on a dues increase?

First, if the vote is at a union meeting, reasonable notice must be given of an intention to vote on the increase. The notice can be through the union newspaper, but it must state explicitly that a vote on a dues increase will be taken.[4] Second, the vote must be by a secret ballot,[5] which has been termed an "absolute protection for the working man, and any vote that dispenses with it is invalid as repugnant to the statute." [6]

Most important, the question must be fairly presented so the member can make a free choice. For example, in one case the vote on a dues increase was linked with a vote on negotiations for a new contract, so that a member could not vote against a dues increase without also voting against a wage increase. The court held that this deprived the members of "the right to a meaningful vote" and ordered the union to disgorge $500,000 which it had collected under the increase.[7] Similarly, linking a dues increase with a pension increase or the settlement of a strike,[8] so that a member must cast a single yes or no vote on a compound question, will invalidate the dues increase.[9]

Are referendums on issues other than increase in union dues regulated by the courts?

Yes. Although the law does not require unions to make decisions by referendum votes,[10] if the union constitution provides for a referendum, then the referendum process will be regulated under three legal rules or principles.

1. The contract theory requires that the referendum be held in accordance with the union constitution. If the constitution requires certain decisions be made by referendum vote, then a decision made in any other way is void; [11] if the constitution requires a secret ballot, a standing vote is no vote at all; [12] if the constitution requires a two-thirds vote, a majority is not enough.

2. The equal-rights clause of the Bill of Rights requires that all members entitled by the constitution to vote have an equal voice in the process. The right to an equal voice goes far beyond the formal right to put pieces of paper in the ballot box. It includes the right to have a substantially equal opportunity to influence the outcome. This equality is measured in practical terms, and is not satisfied by mere form, as some of the following questions and answers will show.

3. Article V of LMRDA imposes on union officers fiduciary duties, and these duties extend to conduct of referendums. Union officers who refuse to submit a question to referendum when required to do so by the constitution, who fail to follow the procedure prescribed by the constitution, or who misrepresent the issue, and thus mislead the members, violate their fiduciary obligation to the union and the members.[13]

What political rights are protected in union referendums by these legal rules or principles?

1. *The right to a fair and open debate.* Union members are entitled to a "free and informed vote . . . not subject to undue influence." [14] In one case, in submit-

ting a new constitution to referendum vote, the officers emphasized popular features of the new constitution and ignored unpopular aspects. When opponents objected that they had not been given access to union publication and mailing lists, the court declared that the officers "had a duty under the LMRDA to conduct a fair referendum." [15] This included the right of those opposed to have opportunity to present their views to the members. The court ordered the officers to make a list of members available to a mailing service so that the opponents could send a letter expressing their views on the issues.[16]

In another case, officers submitted a proposal of merger with another union to referendum vote. However, the letter accompanying the ballot did not contain the full merger agreement, leaving out references to the per-capita tax and other important aspects. The court held that this violated both the equal-rights clause and the fiduciary-obligation title. Any right to vote protected by the equal rights clause, said the court, "must be the right to a meaningful vote. . . . A meaningful vote is not a deliberately uninformed vote, because as such there is no choice. . . . It would be chimerical to hold that Congress guaranteed an equal right to vote on union affairs without requiring that the processes of enlightenment be kept open." Also, the fiduciary duties of union officers "must include the duty to keep the membership informed on matters which they, the rank and file, must decide . . . to see that the lines of communications and dissemination are kept open and working, especially as to matters on which the members will be asked to vote." To the officers' defense that they had only good intentions, the court responded, "The clear policy of the act is to bid farewell to the regime of benevolent well-meaning autocrats, and to give favor to a system of union democracy with its concomitants of free choice and self-determination." [17]

In another merger referendum, the court ordered the union to mail to all members an issue of the union newspaper setting out the full merger agreement, a copy of the constitution of the union with which the merger was proposed, and a sample ballot. In addition, the court ordered the union to provide a special supplement of eight pages devoted to discussion of the views of the proponents and opponents of the merger, with each side given equal space.[18]

2. *The right to a fair choice.* The ballot must be framed so as to give members a meaningful choice. Shortly after passage of the LMRDA, the Machinists Union held a referendum vote on forty-seven amendments to its constitution. The ballot was accompanied by a circular stating that these changes were necessary because of the LMRDA, although many of them were not in fact mandatory. The court held that those actually needed for the union to conform to the LMRDA should have been voted on separately, and that to lump all of the changes together for a single vote "imparted to the members an almost 'forced choice' method of voting." The right to vote is "not a mere naked right to cast a ballot. . . . those who make up the management of the union may not submit amendments for referendum to membership in any way they wish." This "might very well open up the way to usurpation of power by union management, which the Court cannot believe was intended by the framers of the Landrum-Griffin Act." [19]

Similarly, when a local union asked for a single yes or no vote on the two questions of whether the local should disaffiliate and whether to make certain changes in the death-benefit fund, the court invalidated the referendum for tying together two separate issues.

Furthermore, the ballot was improper because it contained "Whereas" clauses that were really arguments for a yes vote.[20]

3. *The right to cast a ballot.* All those entitled by the union constitution to vote, and no others, must be given a fair and equal opportunity to cast a ballot. The courts have regulated membership votes in detail to secure this right.[21] Where members claimed that officers were about to submit the terms of a new agreement to binding arbitration without a ratification vote, the court enjoined arbitration until there was such a vote, ordered that notice of the ratification meeting be given fifteen days in advance along with a summary of the items to be arbitrated, barred members not covered by the contract from the meeting, authorized those bringing the suit to stand at the entrances to make sure that only those entitled to vote entered and to have observers at the counting of the votes, required that at least two hours be allowed at the meeting to discuss the contract and that open microphones be available to speakers who should alternate pro and con, and prescribed that voting should be by division of the house.[22] When voting is by mail, the courts have provided equally detailed protection of the process.[23]

Who is entitled to vote on a particular issue is governed by the union constitution, so long as it is reasonable. Thus, those not working at the trade may be denied the vote on wage scales, but supervisor members cannot be denied the vote on a change of a death benefit fund that includes them.[24]

4. *The right to an honest count.* Counting of ballots improperly cast or miscounting of the ballot violates express or implied provisions of the union constitution. It also violates the equal-rights clause because it dilutes the votes of other members, depriving them of the

effectiveness of their votes, and it violates the fiduciary obligation of those responsible.[25]

Can a union member insist that his local union hold a meeting?

In most cases, yes. Most union constitutions provide that local union meetings shall be held monthly or at specified times. In addition, some provide that special meetings can be called by a petition of a certain number of members. These constitutional provisions can be legally enforced, and courts can order officers to call such meetings.[26]

The LMRDA does not require local unions to hold meetings; indeed, it does not even require unions to have local unions. However, if the constitution provides for local unions with any authority to make decisions or power of self-government, and those decisions are made in meetings, then a member should have a right under the statute to have a meeting held. The equal-rights clause guarantees "equal rights . . . to attend membership meetings and to participate in the deliberations and voting upon the business of such meetings." While the law is not settled on this point, refusal to call a meeting to enable members to participate in making decisions appears to be as much a violation of the equal-rights clause as the refusal to hold a referendum to make decisions required to be made by referendum.[27] In effect, this deprives a member of her right to vote on decisions to be made in meetings and permits union officers to usurp the power to make those decisions. The free-speech clause guarantees every member the right "to express at meetings of the labor organization his views upon candidates in an election of the labor organization or upon any business properly before the meeting." Refusal to call meetings in accordance with union rules deprives members of this aspect of freedom of speech.

The union, through its constitution, can determine what decisions shall be made in local union meetings and when those meetings are to be held, but refusal of the officers to hold such meetings totally destroys the democratic process that these provisions in the constitution are designed to protect.

What protection is given to members to speak at union meetings?

First, every member must be given an equal right to speak and make motions at the union meeting. Recognition of one member to nominate one candidate, but refusal to recognize another member to nominate another candidate, is obviously denial of equal rights to nominate.[28] Denying a member the right to make a motion that is in order and refusing to allow a vote on the motion are also denials of equal rights.

Second, the right to free and open debate is protected. A chairman's refusal to allow a member to speak because of his views is a plain violation of the free-speech clause. Allowing other members to shout him down, physically silence him, or otherwise prevent his being heard is equally a denial of free speech.[29] The failure to maintain order so that those who seek to speak can be heard deprives all members of their right to express their views and participate in the business of the meeting.[30] This does not mean that every member must be allowed to speak on any issue and without end. The union must get its business done. The right to speak is subject to the union's "established and reasonable rules" for the conduct of meetings.

How broad is the protection of freedom of speech and assembly under the free-speech clause?

The guarantees of the free-speech clause are cast in broadest terms: "Every member . . . shall have the right to meet and assemble freely with other members; and to express any views, arguments and opinions. . . ." These rights, however, are subject to a proviso "that nothing herein shall be construed to impair the right of a labor organization to adopt and enforce reasonable rules as to the responsibility of every member toward the organization as an institution and to his refraining from conduct that would interfere with its performance of its legal or contractual obligations."

Despite this proviso, the courts have given the rights guaranteed by the free-speech clause as broad protection as the rights of freedom of speech and assembly under the First Amendment. The union can no more curtail the speech and assembly of its members than government can curtail the speech and assembly of its citizens. Indeed, unions may be able to impose even less restriction on speech and assembly than may government.

Members are protected in criticizing union officers, even though the criticism is claimed to be "personally motivated statements of untruth," and members may freely advocate changes in union policies, even though this creates discontent, dissension, and turmoil in the union.[31] To the union's argument that such activities could be curtailed under the proviso because they violated the member's responsibility to the union as an institution, the answer has been, "This court does not believe that challenge to a union official's integrity to be an act of disloyalty to the union. Just the opposite, it is the duty of the individual union member to speak out about apparent and possible improprieties."[32] To the argument that there is a public interest in promoting solidarity in unions in their dealing with employers, the answer has been, "Congress weighed this factor and decided that the desirability of protecting the democratic process within the unions outweighs any possible weakening of unions in their dealing with employers which may result from freer expression of opinions within the union." [33]

A member of the Musicians Union was expelled for distributing leaflets urging members not to pay a tax levied by the union on the claim that it was unlawful, although this had not been adjudicated. The union justified the expulsion on the grounds that urging members not to pay dues would "undermine the very existence of the Local," and violated the member's responsibility to the union. The court, however, held that this was protected speech. Urging members not to pay was a rational way of testing the validity of the tax and forcing a change in union policy. Furthermore, "A member's responsibility to his union as an institution surely cannot include any obligation to sit idly by while the union follows a course of conduct which he reasonably believes is illegal." [34]

Although free speech is most often curbed by disciplining or threatening to discipline those who speak, other encroachments on free exercise of the rights guaranteed by the free-speech clause are equally forbidden. A member of the National Maritime Union distributed in the union hiring hall a leaflet protesting the policies of the union president. When he persisted after being warned that posted notices prohibited such distribution, police were called and he was arrested for criminal trespass. The court rejected the union's claim that distribution of literature in the hall generated arguments that often resulted in fights, and held that having the member arrested violated his free-speech rights.[35] Similarly, silencing a member by threats of physical harm or other coercive measures violates the free-speech clause.

Can a union member be disciplined for speech that defames union officers or union members?

No. Unions cannot try members for defamatory statements, even though those statements would not be protected under the First Amendment. A member of the Painters Union accused the local president with misuse of union funds, and in leaflets branded him as a "petty robber." He was charged with "slandering union officers" with "unsupported accusations," tried by the union trial board, found guilty, and barred from participation in union affairs for five years. The court refused to follow the analogy of the First Amendment and allow unions to punish defamation, because union tribunals are not qualified to decide whether a statement is defamatory or not. They are not "disinterested tribunals" to which the "alleged defamer can look for an impartial review of his 'crime.' " They are made up of laymen "to which the delicate problems of falsehood, privilege and fair comment were not familiar" and their procedure is "peculiarly unsuited for drawing the fine line between criticism and comment."

It was "clearly in the interest of proper and honest management of union affairs to permit members to question the manner in which the union's officials handle the union's funds." That interest would be frustrated if the union could "compel each dissatisfied and questioning member to draw, at the peril of union discipline, the tenuous line between what is libelous and what is not," particularly when criticism of handling union funds is always likely to be viewed by union officers as defamatory. "The Congress has decided that it is in the public interest that unions be democratically governed and that toward that end that discussion should be free and untrammeled, and that reprisals within the union for the expression of views should be prohibited." [36]

Libelous statements may be made the basis of civil suits in the courts, but the union may not discipline a member on a finding by its trial board that such statements are libelous.[37] This is true even though the charges are made maliciously and without any foundation in fact.[38] In one case, the union hearing officer found that the charges of misuse of funds were "reckless and unfounded, calculated to create dissension among the union membership and designed to disrupt the orderly functioning of the union." The court, however, barred any discipline, saying, "If unions could discipline such speech on the grounds that it weakened their power as an institution, this safeguard would be rendered entirely ephemeral and ineffective." [39]

What limits are there on the right to protest the union's collective-bargaining policy?

A member can be expelled or fined for going to work during a strike, exceeding production limits established by the union, and engaging in a wildcat strike. He cannot escape discipline by saying that his conduct was "symbolic speech" to protest union policies. Beyond this, however, the free-speech protection is very broad.

During a strike, a number of members met to discuss how to end the strike and appointed a committee to discuss the matter with union officers. One of them was charged with "undermining the union negotiating committee" and fined $2,000. This violated both the freedom of speech and freedom of assembly of the members.[40] In another case, after a strike was settled, a member criticized both the strike and the settlement in a nasty letter sent to the employer and various newspapers and public officials. He said that the strike was illegal, unauthorized, and in violation of contract, that intimidation had been used, and that the settlement was no "victory." The court refused to let the union impose and collect a fine against the member for his conduct. "Freedom of speech," said the court, "is protected outside the union hall as well as within"; there was no showing that the speech interfered with any contractual or legal obligation or that it interfered with concluding a settlement.[41]

In a most graphic case, a union steward had condoned a wildcat strike. After the union got the employees back to work, he was discharged, whereupon he picketed the plant with his wife and children and caused a second wildcat, which the union again succeeded in ending. He then notified various newspapers of his intention to "sit in" at the union offices, which he did, and was interviewed by what the opinion characterized as the "Revolutionary Communist Newspaper" of the Progressive Labor Party, to which he belonged. The story was published, along with pictures and his charge that the union leaders were spineless. He was charged with instigating a work stoppage, engaging in a sit-in, and causing the printing of a libelous article, which was used to ridicule the union by an employer the union was seeking to organize. There was a general verdict of guilty on all these charges and he was expelled. The court held that causing the article to be published was protected as free speech. even though it accused the officers of collusion with the employer and praised the workers for their militancy, because "the union's response to laid-off or discharged workers is a most basic issue to a union member, and speech in dealing with this issue is protected by the Act." Because the union proceedings did not make clear whether his expulsion was based on this charge or the wildcat-strike charge, he was ordered reinstated in the union.[42]

Can a union member be disciplined for supporting a rival union in a representation election?

Yes, but if he is fined, the union cannot sue him to collect the fine. Dual unionism has been a traditional ground for expulsion from a union, and any support of a rival union may be considered a violation of the member's responsibility to the union as an institution. The union can protect itself from having someone loyal to a competing union within its ranks, and to do this it can expel him from the union or bar him from participating in union decisions.[43]

Supporting a competing union in an NLRB election is entitled to special protection in order to insure the employees' free choice of their bargaining representative. However, expelling a member because he supports a rival union leaves him free to support the union he prefers; it only limits his membership to the union he supports. In contrast, fining a member who supports a competing union and then suing him in court to collect the fine penalizes the member in monetary terms for exercising freedom of choice. Fines enforced by a court coerce dissatisfied employees to silence and destroy the right to freely choose representatives, guaranteed by Section 7 of the NLRA. At the same time, collecting such fines serves no legitimate purpose of the union, for it does not protect the union from having enemies within, but instead requires that they stay within and insures their deeper enmity. A union rule that enforces fines against members who seek a change of bargaining representative is simply not a "reasonable rule" as to the member's responsibility to the union.[44]

Do members have a right to form factional groups or caucuses within the union?

Yes. The free-speech clause protects freedom of assembly, expressly guaranteeing "the right to meet and assemble freely with other members." This was deliberately included in the Bill of Rights to protect members in forming opposition groups, factions, or caucuses within the union, for only through such groups can members effectively participate in the union's political processes. As one court said, "To permit a union to punish its members for meeting and discussing affairs of the union would be to deny the very purpose of the Bill of Rights." [45]

Are broad or vague disciplinary provisions void because of their "chilling effect" on freedom of speech and assembly?

Generally not. A union may describe offenses in general terms—such as "undermining wage standards," [46] or "conduct unbecoming a union member." [47] Even though such a provision may have a "chilling effect" upon its members—by discouraging them from certain conduct because they cannot be sure if the conduct violates the rule—such a vague rule is permissible as long as it is not actually applied in a way which violates the LMRDA.

However, where the union repeatedly uses a provision to punish protected conduct, the court can permanently enjoin any further prosecutions under that provision.[48] For example, officers of The Mine Workers Union had filed a series of disciplinary charges against supporters of opposing candidates, charging them with violating a clause prohibiting "dishonest or questionable practices to secure the election or defeat of a candidate." The court held that this clause was so vague that a member exercising rights guaranteed by the LMRDA would be in peril of violating the clause and "might well refrain from taking full advantage of his rights." The officers, by their actions, had demonstrated their determination to use the provision to harass and intimidate the opposition. The only way to protect statutory rights was to enjoin prosecutions under the vague provision.[49]

Enjoining prosecution even before the union has had a trial obviously runs counter to the general rule that the courts will not intervene before internal union appeals are exhausted. However, where freedoms of speech and assembly are at stake, the courts have been quite ready to find reasons for excusing exhaustion of internal appeals.[50] In many cases, the appeal is to the very officers who have been criticized or who were opposed in the election, so the appeal would be futile.[51] In others the discipline may bar the member from participating in an upcoming union election or in discussions of a new collective agreement, and the court finds that this is irreparable injury. But some courts have simply declared that where free-speech rights are involved, the reasons for requiring exhaustion are absent.[52]

Union tribunals may be helpful to the court in interpreting the union's rules, but they have "no special expertise in determining First Amendment rights or their statutory analogs." [53] Nor will requiring exhaustion in such cases conserve much judicial energy, for the legal issues are usually so clear that immediate judicial determination will require little energy. To delay would be to deprive members of significant rights that cannot be remedied by money damages.[54]

NOTES

1. Musicians Union v. Wittstein, 379 U.S. 171 (1964).
2. Gordon v. Laborers Union, 490 F.2d 133 (10th Cir. 1973).

3. Rota v. Brotherhood of Railway, Airline and Steamship Clerks, 489 F.2d 998 (7th Cir. 1973).
4. Gates v. Dalton, 90 LRRM 2368 (E.D. N.Y. 1975).
5. Steib v. Longshoremen Local 1497, 436 F.2d 1101 (5th Cir. 1971).
6. White v. King, 319 F.Supp. 122, 124, 125 (E.D. La. 1970).
7. Sertic v. Carpenters Dist. Council, 423 F.2d 515, 521 (6th Cir. 1970).
8. White v. King, *supra* note 6.
9. Gates v. Dalton, *supra* note 4.
10. Vestal v. Teamsters Union, 81 LRRM 2732 (D.C. Cir. 1972).
11. Taxi Rank & File Coalition v. Van Arsdale, 86 LRRM 2362 (S.D. N.Y. 1974).
12. Britt v. Peninsula Shipbuilders Ass'n, 307 F.Supp. 3 (E.D. Va. 1969).
13. Keck v. Employees Independent Ass'n, 388 F.Supp. 243 (E.D. Pa. 1974).
14. Cefalo v. Moffett, 449 F.2d 1193, 1199 (D.C. Cir. 1971).
15. Sheldon v. O'Callaghan, 497 F.2d 1276, 1282 (2nd Cir. 1974).
16. *Ibid.*
17. Blanchard v. Johnson, 388 F.Supp. 208, 215 (N.D. Ohio 1974).
18. Cefalo v. Moffett, *supra* note 14.
19. Young v. Hayes, 195 F.Supp. 911, 916 (D.D.C. 1961).
20. Local 13410, Mine Workers v. Mine Workers Union 325 F.Supp. 1107 (D.D.C. 1971).
21. Vestal v. Teamsters Union, 245 F.Supp. 623 (M.D. Tenn. 1965).
22. Taxi Rank & File Coalition v. Van Arsdale, 86 LRRM 2359 (S.D. N.Y. 1973).
23. Cefalo v. Moffett, *supra* note 14.
24. Local 13410, UMWA v. UMWA, *supra* note 20.
25. Stettner v. Printing Pressmen Union, 278 F.Supp. 675 (E.D. Tenn. 1967).

26. Capolino v. Matranga, 33 A.D. 2d 33 (1969), *modified and aff'd*, 25 N.Y. 2d 730 (1969).
27. *But see* Yanity v. Benware, 376 F.2d 197 (2nd Cir. 1967).
28. Burch v. Machinists Union, 454 F.2d 1170 (5th Cir. 1971).
29. Scovile v. Watson, 338 F.2d 678 (7th Cir. 1964).
30. Allen v. Iron Workers Local 192, 47 LRRM 2214 (N.D. Ala. 1960).
31. Burns v. Painters Local 1503, 90 LRRM 2824, 2827 (D.C. Conn. 1975).
32. Nix v. Machinists Union, Fulton Lodge 2, 83 LRRM 2478, 2480 (N.D. Ga. 1972), *aff'd.* 479 F.2d 382 (5th Cir. 1973).
33. Salzhandler v. Caputo, 316 F.2d 445, 451 (2nd Cir. 1963).
34. Farowitz v. Musicians Union, 330 F.2d 992, 1002 (2nd Cir. 1964).
35. Morrisey v. National Maritime Union, 397 F Supp. 659 (S.D. N.Y. 1975).
36. Salzhandler v. Caputo, *supra* note 33, at 451.
37. Fulton Lodge 2, International Ass'n of Machinists v. Nix, 415 F.2d 212 (5th Cir. 1969).
38. Cole v. Hall, 339 F.2d 881 (2d. Cir. 1965), *aff'd.* 412 U.S. 1 (1973); Burns v. Painters Local 1503, *supra* note 31; Nix v. Machinists Union, Fulton Lodge 2, *supra* note 32.
39. Giordani v. Upholsterers Union, 403 F.2d 85, 89–90 (2nd Cir. 1968).
40. Kuebler v. Lithographers & Photo-Engravers Local 24-P, 473 F.2d 359 (6th Cir. 1973).
41. Farnum v. Kurtz, 72 LRRM 2794 (Cal. Super. Ct. App. Div. 1969).
42. Pearl v. Tarantola, 361 F. Supp. 288, 293 (S.D. N.Y. 1973).
43. Sawyers v. Grand Lodge, Machinists, 279 F. Supp. 747 (E.D. Mo. 1967).
44. Airline Maintenance Lodge 702, IAMAW v. Loudermilk, 444 F.2d 719 (5th Cir. 1971).

45. Kuebler v. Lithographers & Photo-Engravers Local 24-P, *supra* note 40, at 364.
46. *Ibid.*
47. International Bhd. of Boilermakers v. Hardeman, 401 U.S. 233 (1971).
48. Clothing Workers Rank & File Comm. v. Clothing Workers Philadelphia Joint Bd., 473 F.2d 1303 (3rd Cir. 1973).
49. Semancik v. Mine Workers Dist. 5, 466 F.2d 144, 154 (3rd Cir. 1972).
50. *But see* Clothing Workers, *supra* note 48.
51. Semancik v. Mine Workers, *supra* note 49; Nix v. Machinists, Fulton Lodge 2, 452 F.2d 794 (5th Cir. 1971).
52. Burns v. Painters Local 1503, *supra* note 31.
53. Pearl v. Tarantola, *supra* note 42.
54. Sheridan v. Liquor Salesmen's Union, Local 2, 303 F. Supp. 999 (S.D. N.Y. 1969).

IV

The Right to Fair and Open Elections

The integrity of the electoral process is a cornerstone of union democracy. The regulation of union elections, including the right of members to run for office and to vote, is spelled out in Title IV of the LMRDA. You should consult the text of Title IV (see Appendix A) as you read this chapter and if you encounter actual problems in union elections. You may also find helpful a manual entitled *Electing Union Officers,* published by the Department of Labor.[1] In addition, the Secretary of Labor has promulgated rules explaining and interpreting several of the provisions of the statute, although these rules do not have the binding legal effect of the statute itself.[2]

The law in this area has developed on a case-by-case basis, with the decision often turning on the particular facts involved. As in the other areas we have discussed, the provisions of the union constitution may significantly affect voting rights.[3]

The voting-rights section of the LMRDA is unique in that the enforcement of these rights is left almost exclusively to the Secretary of Labor.[4] Thus, much of the law in this area is developed initially by administrative decisions—subject, of course, to review and enforcement in the courts.[5] Moreover, an individual usually cannot move directly into the court to protect his right to vote, but must rely upon the Secretary of Labor. As with other sections of the LMRDA, the complaining member must first exhaust his internal review procedure, but if an acceptable decision is not reached by the union within three months, he is free to file a complaint with the Secretary of Labor.[6]

Numerous issues can arise under Title IV, and we emphasize that the resolution of any given case depends upon the particular facts presented. These questions and answers provide only guidelines. Legal assistance or inquiry to the Department of Labor may be appropriate if actual problems arise.

The complaining member should understand that there is no assurance that the Secretary of Labor will find merit in his complaint. The Secretary of Labor's function is not only to enforce the rights of union members, but to screen out those complaints which he deems frivolous, in order to protect unions from unnecessary litigation and judicial interference with their elections. As the Supreme Court has said, the secretary has the obligation to protect the "vital public interest in assuring free and democratic elections that transcends the narrower interest of the complaining union member."[7] The complaining member may not be satisfied with the way in which the secretary handles his complaint, for, as the court also observed, "even if the Secretary is performing his duties, broadly conceived, as well as can be expected, the union member may have a valid complaint about the performance of 'his lawyer.'"[8]

Must a union hold elections?

Yes. If the union has some form of governing body, elections will be required under the LMRDA. The statute requires that "the officers" of a labor organization be elected.[9] An officer is generally considered to be a person who exercises executive functions or who determines policy. Whether a business agent is to be treated as an officer who is required to be elected, or as an employee of the union who may be appointed, presents a close factual question.[10]

How often must such elections be held?

At least once every three years in the case of officers of the local union, every four years for officers of intermediate bodies, and every five years for national or international officers.[11] Examples of an intermediate body include a system board or a joint board that operates on a level between the local and the national or international union.

Is secret balloting required?

A secret-ballot election is required only in the case of elections in a local labor organization.[12] Officers of the national or international union may be elected by secret ballot, or, depending upon the union constitution, may be chosen at a convention by delegates who are in turn elected by secret ballot.[13] If a labor union has an intermediate body, its officers may be elected by secret-ballot election of the members or by officers who have been elected by secret ballot.[14]

What eligibility requirements may a union impose for holding office?

The union has a limited right to impose eligibility requirements for holding office. The LMRDA provides that "every member in good standing shall be eligible to be a candidate and to hold office." However, the act qualifies this right by allowing the union to establish "reasonable qualifications uniformly imposed." [15] This is a double requirement. A valid restriction on eligibility to hold office must not only be applied evenhandedly to all potential candidates, but must be "reasonable." As you would expect, there has been much litigation on the question of what is a "reasonable" qualification for office.

In a leading case on eligibility requirements, the Supreme Court provided useful guidance.[16] A bylaw of a local union limited eligibility for major elective offices to those union members who had previously held some lesser elective office within the union. The union argued that this requirement insured that those elected would be familiar with the workings of the local by serving in lesser offices. The Court declared the rule invalid, stating that it was up to the voter and not the union to decide whether a particular candidate was qualified for office. The Court also noted that the union's rules would make some 93 percent of the members ineligible for office, and that such a massive disqualification could hardly be considered reasonable. The Court explained:

Congress plainly did not intend that the authorization in Sec. 401(e) of "reasonable qualifications uniformly imposed" should be given a broad reach. The contrary is implicit. . . . Unduly restrictive candidacy qualifications can result in the abuses of entrenched leadership that the LMRDA was expressly enacted to curb. The check of democratic elections as a preventive measure is seriously impaired by candidacy qualifications which substantially deplete the ranks of those who might run in opposition to incumbents.[17]

In another case, recently decided by the Supreme Court, the union constitution limited eligibility for office to members who had attended at least one-half of the regular meetings of the local for three years prior to the election. In the particular local involved, only 23 of the local's approximately 660 members satisfied this requirement, and of these, 9 were incumbent officers. Thus, the eligibility requirement disqualified over 96 per cent of the union's members. The union argued that the rule served valid union purposes, was not burdensome, and had not served to entrench the existing leadership. The Court disagreed, holding that the "antidemocratic effects" of this eligibility rule outweighed any justification for it, and that the disqualification of so many members "obviously severely restricts the free choice of the membership in selecting its leaders." [18]

The courts have thrown out other eligibility requirements that unreasonably hampered the right to run for office. In one case a union rule required a candidate to transfer from a branch local to the parent local, at an additional cost of from $75 to $90, to be eligible to run for office. The court found no legitimate purpose for this requirement, which imposed an unreasonable financial burden on the right to run for office.[19]

But a union may bar a person from running for office if he belongs to a rival labor organization or holds a supervisory position in his employment, as either status may be inconsistent with the union's best interests.[20] In addition, the LMRDA expressly provides that a union may deny the right to run to a member who is barred from holding office on one of the grounds listed in Section 504 of the act—for example, conviction for certain crimes.[21]

What are the procedures for nominating candidates?

The LMRDA requires that "a reasonable opportunity shall be given for the nomination of candidates." The actual procedures for nominating candidates may be determined by the union, so long as they do not unreasonably burden the member's right to nominate candidates and run for office. For example, a union constitution required that a candidate secure nominating petitions from five local unions and submit them by a certain date. The union barred his candidacy when the secretary of one of the locals failed to send in a petition to the parent union on time. The court held that the member could not be denied the right to run for office where the delay was the fault of a union officer and not the individual. The court went further and declared the procedure defective on its face because of the potential for abuse by local union officials in not transmitting petitions to the parent union.[22]

The union must give members reasonable and timely notice of when and where nominations must be made. It may not require potential candidates to declare their candidacy before the actual nominations are due, nor may it require candidates to pay a filing fee.[23] Similarly, the procedures for placing names in nomination must not be manipulated or designed to frustrate potential candidates. Thus, a union violated the act by locking the doors and starting a nominating meeting precisely on time when it knew that a member standing in the hall wished to nominate a candidate.[24]

May a union impose restrictions upon the right to vote?

Generally, no. The LMRDA provides that "each member in good standing shall be entitled to one vote." [25] While a union is generally not compelled to admit anyone to membership, once it admits a person it may not restrict her right to vote, except in limited circumstances. Unlike the right to run for office, the statute does not allow for "reasonable qualifications" upon the right to vote. The union is permitted under Section 101(a)(1) of the LMRDA to make "reasonable rules and regulations" concerning voting rights, but its discretion is much more limited than when it prescribes qualifications for holding office. Generally, the union may impose a brief membership requirement—usually under a year—as a condition of voting. And it may require the member to have paid up his dues in order to vote. Naturally, to be valid, these rules must be applied uniformly.[26]

What rights does the LMRDA give a candidate in campaigning for office?

The union is required to maintain a list of the names and last known addresses of all persons who are members of the union in all cases in which a collective-bargaining agreement requires union membership as a condition of employment. A candidate is entitled to inspect this list once within thirty days of the election.[27] However, the candidate may not copy the list, except under circumstances discussed shortly. Congress was reluctant to require full copying of the list because unions expressed a fear that the lists might be used by rival employers and others to harm the union.[28]

The candidate may require the union to distribute her campaign literature by mail or otherwise to all members in good standing, at the candidate's expense.[29] The union does not have the right to censor or reject any of this material, even if it believes it to be untrue or slanderous.[30] The right to inspect the membership list, discussed in the previous paragraph, helps assure that the union will provide for full distribution of the materials.

In addition to the two specific rights just discussed, of inspection and distribution, the LMRDA gives the candidate an important tool by requiring equal treatment of all candidates in using membership lists and distributing literature.[31] This means that if one candidate, such as an incumbent officer, copies or uses the membership list to distribute his materials, the union must give all other candidates the same right to use the list.[32] More significantly, if the union permits one candidate to publish campaign materials free of charge in the union newspaper, it must provide the same right to other candidates.[33] This is a vital safeguard where the union is actively promoting the candidacy of a particular person.

Where the election involves a candidate who is already in office, this rule becomes difficult to apply, for the union will normally provide some coverage in its newspaper of the activities of its current leaders. In this respect the incumbent enjoys the same election advantage as an incumbent president of the United States by virtue of the wide news coverage of his activities. Yet the courts have not hesitated to find a violation where the coverage of the incumbent's activities went beyond normal newsworthy items and was really a device to promote his candidacy. This is well illustrated by the election in the Mine Workers Union between the incumbent Boyle and the challenger Yablonski. While conceding that at bottom a "judgment decision" is involved, the court stated: "A line must be drawn between the use of the Journal to report the activities of defendant Boyle as President, which is permissible, and the use of the Journal, in such a way in reporting such activities as to promote the candidacy of such defendant."[34] The Court found excessive coverage of Boyle's activities in relation to their newsworthiness, and an unexplained absence of any reference to Yablonski, who held an important position within the union.

These decisions involve delicate judgments affecting freedom of the press, and courts are reluctant to infringe upon First Amendment rights. Thus, in the Yablonski-Boyle litigation the court very carefully avoided a remedy that would interfere with the union's freedom of the press. It merely ordered the union to provide Yablonski with an equal right to space whenever it gave coverage to Boyle as a candidate; it rejected Yablonski's requested relief that the union be compelled to print specific materials concerning his candidacy.

May union money be used to support a particular candidate?

No. The LMRDA provides that no monies received by the union in the form of dues, assessments, or similar levy may be utilized to promote the candidacy of any person. This prohibition is very broad and reaches even minimal expenditures. Thus, it bans union officers or paid union employees from campaigning for a candidate, even for themselves, during paid working time, and prohibits the use of an office duplicating machine to produce campaign literature. Violations of this rule may invalidate the election.[35] Candidates, whether or not they are presently union officers, may of course raise campaign funds by soliciting union members, but the contributions must be voluntary; union officers can engage in such fund-raising only on their own time.[36] Outsiders may also contribute money or effort to a candidacy, with one exception—an employer is not permitted to contribute.[37]

A delicate line is again drawn between actual support of candidates and mere accommodation of their campaign needs. For example, if a union gives all candidates free space in its newspaper, this would satisfy the provision of the act requiring equal treatment of candidates, but would technically violate the prohibition against the use of union monies to support candidates. Most courts have allowed unions, within reason, to give all candidates free space in union newspapers. This serves the basic purpose of Section 401(c) of the statute in providing a fair election with free and open debate that enables members to cast a knowledgeable vote.[38] However, one court has said that even if these funds are made available to all candidates, the section is nevertheless violated.[39]

What rules govern the conduct of the balloting itself?
The LMRDA contains both general and specific provisions insuring that the election will be conducted fairly. The general requirement is that "adequate safeguards to insure a fair election shall be provided." [40] The specific protections include:

1. The requirement that each member of the union be mailed an election notice not less than fifteen days prior to the election.[41]
2. The requirement of secret balloting.[42]
3. The right of a candidate to have an observer at the polls and at the counting of the ballots.[43]
4. The requirement that ballots and records of the election be preserved for one year.[44]
5. The requirement that votes be cast and counted separately within each local and the results be published separately.[45] This last requirement is designed to make it easier for a member to determine whether election misconduct may have occurred, for if there is misconduct that affects the vote, it is

likely to show up in the count of the particular local ballots.

Must the member actually vote by secret ballot or is it enough that he is given the opportunity to vote by secret ballot?

While the LMRDA is not entirely clear on this point, the prevailing case law holds that it is not enough that a secret ballot is available to the member; rather, the union must make sure that all voters use that procedure. This is a sensible rule, for a secret ballot is defined in the act as one that insures that the voter's choice cannot be identified.[46] In one case voters were allowed to mark their ballots in the open, in the presence of other voters and observers.[47] While provision was made for a voter to mark his ballot in private, the court concluded that a voter who wanted to do this would probably call attention to himself and indicate to others how he intended to vote.

Must the union provide absentee ballots for those unable to vote in person?

The LMRDA makes no provision for absentee ballots, and the case law is unsettled on this subject. Where a substantial number of members are away from the polling place for long periods of time and where it is physically impossible for large numbers of them to vote in person, as in the maritime industry, an absentee ballot will be required.[48] But where the member may vote in person without too much inconvenience, or has voluntarily moved away, as in the case of retirees, an absentee ballot will not be required, particularly if the polls are kept open for several days to allow those on out-of-town assignments, such as truckdrivers, to return to vote.[49] Of course if the union constitution or bylaws require that absentee ballots be provided, this requirement must be followed.

What if the instructions on the ballot are confusing or the ballot is not marked clearly?

The courts have attempted to decide these issues on the basis of common sense and fairness, after examining the facts carefully. Confusing instructions might void the election if the court is convinced that voters were misled.[50] As for marking of ballots, in one case an impartial committee in charge of counting ballots decided to count all choices on the ballot that were clearly marked and to reject all choices not clearly marked. It decided not to reject a ballot altogether where only some of the choices were unclearly marked. The court upheld this as reasonable.[51]

What is entailed by the right to have an observer at the polls?

Basically, the observer must be given the opportunity to verify that only eligible voters cast a ballot and that all ballots of eligible voters, and no other ballots, are counted. The observer is entitled to a list of eligible voters. He has a right to be present when voters receive ballots and place them in the box and must be given the opportunity to challenge those ballots that he thinks are cast by ineligible voters.[52] These challenged ballots must be kept apart from other ballots.[53] The observer has a right to oversee the sealing of the ballot box at the conclusion of voting, to observe that it is placed in custody, to be present when the ballot box is opened, and to see each ballot as it is counted. Evidence of tampering with the ballot box is grounds to invalidate the election.[54]

What procedures are available to enforce the right to a fair and open election?

There are basically two procedures. First, a suit may be brought prior to an election to correct or prevent certain existing or threatened violations. Second, a complaint may be filed with the Secretary of Labor after an election challenging the validity of the election; in appropriate cases he can bring a suit to set the election aside and direct a new one.

In what situations can a suit be brought prior to an election?

Under the LMRDA this procedure is limited to three types of situations:

1. Failure of the union to comply with the right of a candidate to have the union distribute campaign literature at his request.
2. Refusal by the union to give a candidate access to the membership lists where there is a union-shop agreement.
3. Discrimination by the union among the candidates with respect to access to mailing lists, and unequal distribution of campaign literature, including giving special coverage in the union newspaper to the activities of the incumbent, but no space to the challenger.[55]

In these cases the objecting candidate may bring suit immediately in the U.S. District Court. The court may not only enjoin the violation, but it may stop the election until the violation has been corrected. Whether the court will hold up the election or allow it to go forward, leaving it to the Secretary of Labor to later determine whether the completed election was valid, is a matter for the discretion of the court. Because postponing an election is disruptive and expensive, the court will not delay the election unless it is satisfied that violations of the act have occurred and that they are serious enough to affect the outcome of the election. On the other hand, postponement may be less disruptive than having a completed election challenged and subsequently rerun; therefore, if the court is convinced that violations will invalidate the election, it may halt the election.[56]

Will an election be allowed to go forward even though there are violations that will clearly invalidate the election?

Yes. If the violations are not within the categories mentioned in the preceding answer, there is no authority under the LMRDA for a court to intervene before the election. And even if the violations fall within those categories, they may be challenged in court only by a candidate for office in the labor union involved. In all cases that do not allege violations of the type discussed in the previous answer, or in which the complaining member is not a candidate for office, the election must go forward. Such violations would include the failure to conduct an election by secret ballot, the failure to insure adequate safeguards at the polling place, the failure to send an election notice to a member, or the union's expenditure of money to support a candidate.[57] After the election, the complaining member may file a complaint with the Secretary of Labor challenging the election. Once the election is held, the only way to challenge it is through the Secretary of Labor.[58]

To illustrate how narrow the preelection remedies are, in a leading case the union had a restrictive eligibility requirement for becoming a candidate. Members of the union brought suit to enjoin the union from holding the election until this requirement was eliminated. The Supreme Court held that however unfair the eligibility requirement might be, the exclusive route for challenging it was through a postelection suit by the Secretary of Labor:

> Reliance on the discretion of the Secretary is in harmony with the general congressional policy to allow unions great latitude in resolving their own internal controversies, and, where that fails, to utilize the agencies of Government most familiar with union problems to aid in bringing about a settlement through discussion before resorting to the courts.[59]

What are the procedures for challenging an election after it is held?

As a first step, the complaining member must exhaust any election-appeal procedures provided by the union constitution that are available within three months.[60] This is to give the union the first opportunity to correct its mistakes. Failure to exhaust these appeals will normally bar the member from any legal relief, but if he can show that the internal appeal would have been futile—for example, because it would have to be made to the officers who won the contested election—then resort to these procedures will be excused.[61]

The second step is to file a complaint with the Secretary of Labor, which must be done within one month from the time the union turns down the final appeal or within one month from the time the three-month exhaustion period expires, whichever comes first.[62] The secretary is charged by the statute with the responsibility for investigating the claim within sixty days—a time limit often not met—and determining whether there is "probable cause" to believe that a violation occurred.[63] If he finds "probable cause" and determines that the case is an appropriate one, he brings suit in the federal district court to set aside the election and hold a new one. The court must decide whether there has been a violation and whether a new election should be held.

Once the Secretary of Labor initiates his court action, does the complaining member, or any other affected person, have any right to intervene in the court proceeding?

Yes. The Supreme Court has held that members affected by the unfair election may intervene in the secretary's suit. They may want to present evidence or develop arguments that they feel the secretary will not adequately cover. But they are limited to dealing with those violations that are part of the secretary's suit; they may not raise matters not covered in the secretary's complaint.[64]

Does the Secretary of Labor move to set the election aside in all cases in which there is a violation of the statute?

No. First of all, the secretary can rely only on violations that were raised by the union member in his internal appeals and in his complaint filed with the secretary, or violations closely related to those complained of. Even though the secretary's investigation may reveal other violations, these may not be relied upon unless the complaining member could not have known of them at the time he filed his complaint. For example, a union member filed a complaint with the Secretary of Labor charging that union facilities had been used to promote the candidacy of the incumbent. The secretary investigated the complaint and added the charge that the union had imposed an unreasonable meeting-attendance requirement as a condition of candidacy. The Supreme Court held that the secretary could not rely upon this additional ground in his suit, for this would defeat the purpose of the exhaustion requirement in the act by not giving the union a chance to change the attendance requirement.[65]

In addition, the secretary must find that the violations "may have affected the outcome of the election"; that is, if it had not been for the violations the election *might* have been won by the losing candidate. Thus, if fifty members are not sent a notice of the election, and the winner's margin of victory is only forty votes, then the violation *might* have affected the outcome. But if the winner's margin is sixty votes, then the violation could not have affected the outcome, and a new election will not be sought by the secretary.[66]

However, if the secretary charges that a member was wrongfully disqualified from running, the election will be set aside even though realistically there was little chance that the disqualified candidate would have won had he been allowed to run. The courts will not weigh the political factors in an election in determining whether the violation may have affected the outcome.[67] Similarly, refusal to send out mailings, misuse of the union newspaper, or other campaign violations will generally be treated as likely to have changed the outcome of the election, unless the union can show convincingly that the outcome would not have been affected by the violations.[68]

Who governs the union while the election is being challenged?

The officers who were elected in the challenged election. The LMRDA specifically provides that the challenged election shall be presumed valid until there is a final court decision invalidating the election; this decision comes only when the court certifies the results of the rerun election.[69] Because of the time spent investigating and trying to work out a settlement with the union, the secretary often does not bring suit until months or even years after the complaint is filed. The litigation, with appeals, may be very lengthy. In a number of cases the full term of office has run and another election has been held before the validity of the earlier one is finally settled. The union is permitted to hold subsequent elections in regular course, even though an earlier one has been challenged. This is permitted because the first election may be upheld, and the union's regular processes should therefore not be disturbed. But even if the subsequent, regular election is entirely fair, the fact that it occurred does not make a suit challenging the first election moot. If the first election is ultimately declared invalid, a rerun election will be ordered even if there has been a subsequent valid election.[70]

What is involved when the court orders a rerun election?

The court generally directs that the election be held under the supervision of the Secretary of Labor. The secretary will generally follow the union's constitutional election procedures, but will make any changes he thinks necessary to insure an open and fair election. The regulation may be quite detailed and the supervision intensive at every stage, or it may be less involved. As the nomination procedures and election campaign develop, either the challengers or the incumbents may ask the secretary for new rules or for changes, or may go to court to obtain what they believe is needed. The court has the ultimate authority and responsibility for determining the conditions under which the new election shall be held.[71]

How effective is this method of enforcement in protecting the right to fair and open elections?

Many think that the existing procedures encourage election violations, because the limited availability of preelection remedies and the slowness of postelection remedies allow the victor to enjoy the fruits of his violations. The Yablonski-Boyle election is often cited as an example of this, for the violations began six months before the election was held, but Boyle continued as president of the Mine Workers for four years after the election. But the magnitude of the Yablonski-Mine Workers litigation, which involved dozens of separate legal proceedings, was attributable in part to the unusual complexity of the problems involved. It was also attributable to the relative uncertainty of the law at that time; the litigation itself was responsible for the development of much of the law in this area.[72] A summary and chronology of the complete Yablonski-Mine Workers litigation appears in Appendix B of this book.

The temptation to violate the law is lessened, however, by the onus and expense which come with a challenged election, and the uncertainty that is created until the matter is adjudicated. Certainly, the extensive use of preelection remedies could get the courts so deeply involved in complex issues that elections might be repeatedly postponed, leaving the incumbent officers in control. Intervention by the Secretary of Labor prior to an election cannot be extensive because he lacks the resources to supervise large numbers of elections closely.

Perhaps the greatest inadequacy in the existing procedures is the lack of confidence on the part of those challenging union elections that the Secretary of Labor will enforce the law impartially and vigorously. Perhaps this view derives from the Secretary of Labor's traditionally close ties with incumbent union leadership. This lack of confidence, along with the delays and burdens attached to litigation, may discourage challengers from asserting their legal rights. And the feeling that their legal rights will not be vindicated may in turn discourage them from challenging incumbent union officers in union elections.

Are there any other ways to challenge and remedy union practices which interfere with a fair election?

Yes. The Yablonski-Boyle election [73] illustrates ways to challenge the union's practices that do not directly involve Title IV. For example, Yablonski was ousted from his office within the union during the election campaign. Such removal was challenged under Title I as a denial of Yablonski's free-speech rights and under Section 609 of the LMRDA, which prohibits discipline of members for exercising any right protected under the act and permits direct judicial intervention to protect such rights. This decision awarded punitive damages.[74] In addition, union members brought suit against the union for restoration of funds improperly spent in support of the incumbent candidates.[75] Other lawsuits dealt with the improper creation of trusteeship of locals, a matter discussed in Chapter V of this book.[76] Finally, and perhaps most significantly, Yablonski's attorneys succeeded in recovering attorneys' fees involved in the entire litigation.[77] The reader should be aware that the litigation just described is unusual, and that the more conventional and limited remedies of Title IV will control in most cases.

Does the LMRDA permit a union to remove an officer who is improperly elected?

It is not clear from the statutory language and reported cases whether a union may utilize its internal discipline procedures to remove an officer who it thinks was improperly elected.[78] It certainly may be argued that the only remedy for unlawful campaign conduct is through a suit by the Secretary of Labor under Title IV. The potential for removal of an elected officer while Title IV proceedings are pending may jeopardize the status of insurgent candidates who have ousted the established leadership more than it threatens the incumbent candidate who wins an election by improper means.

NOTES

1. U. S. Dep't of Labor, Electing Union Officers (1967).
2. These regulations are found in Volume 29 of the *Code of Federal Regulations,* cited in these footnotes as 29 C.F.R., followed by the appropriate regulation number.
3. LMRDA § 403.
4. LMRDA § 402; compare LMRDA § 401(c).
5. LMRDA §§ 402(b), (c).
6. LMRDA § 401(a).
7. Trbovich v. Mine Workers Union, 404 U.S. 528, 539 (1972).
8. *Ibid.*
9. LMRDA §§ 401(a), (b).
10. LMRDA § 3(q.); Secretary of Labor's Regulations, 29 C.F.R. 452.16–21.
11. LMRDA §§ 401(a), (b), (d).
12. LMRDA § 401(b).
13. LMRDA § 401(a).
14. LMRDA § 401(d).
15. LMRDA § 401(e).
16. Wirtz v. Hotel Employees Union, 391 U.S. 492 (1968).
17. *Ibid.* at 499.

18. Steelworkers Union v. Usery, 429 U.S. 305 (1977).
19. Hodgson v. Local 18, Operating Engineers, 440 F.2d 485 (6th Cir. 1971).
20. Secretary of Labor's Regulations, 29 C.F.R. 452.44, .47.
21. LMRDA §§ 401(e) and 504. *See* United States v. Brown, 381 U.S. 437 (S.Ct. declaring Sec. 504 unconstitutional insofar as it imposes criminal sanctions on Communist Party members for holding union office). *Compare* Driscoll v. Operating Engineers Local 139, 484 F.2d 682 (7th Cir. 1973), which upheld a union rule disqualifying from office a member who declined to sign an affidavit of nonaffiliation with the Communist Party.
22. Hodgson v. District 6, Mine Workers, 474 F.2d 940 (6th Cir. 1973).
23. Secretary of Labor's Regulations, 29 C.F.R. 452.52, .56, .57.
24. Garrett v. Dorosh, 77 LRRM 2650 (E.D. Mich. 1971).
25. LMRDA § 401(e).
26. Secretary of Labor's Regulations, 29 C.F.R. 452.86, .88. The matter of admission to membership is discussed in Chapter II. LMRDA 3(o) defines a member in good standing as one who has "fulfilled the requirements for membership" who has not voluntarily withdrawn from membership. One ceases to be a member if he has been suspended or expelled in accordance with proper procedures.
27. LMRDA § 401(c).
28. COX, BOK, & GORMAN, CASES ON LABOR LAW 1271 (1977).
29. LMRDA § 401(c).
30. Backo v. Carpenters Union, 438 F.2d 176 (2nd Cir. 1970).
31. LMRDA § 401(c).
32. Shultz v. Radio Officers Union, 344 F. Supp. 58 (S.D. N.Y. 1972).

33. Hodgson v. Liquor Salesmen's Union, 444 F.2d 1344 (2nd Cir. 1971).

34. Yablonski v. Mine Workers Union, 305 F. Supp. 868, 871 (D.D.C. 1969).

35. Shultz v. Local 6799, Steelworkers, 426 F.2d 969 (9th Cir. 1970), aff'd, 403 U.S. 333 (1971); Hodgson v. Liquor Salesmen's Union, 444 F.2d 1344, 1350 (2nd Cir. 1971).

36. Secretary of Labor's Regulations, 29 C.F.R. 452.76.

37. LMRDA § 402(g).

38. See Secretary of Labor's Regulations, 29 C.F.R. 452.73–.75.

39. Shultz v. Local 6799, Steelworkers, supra note 35.

40. LMRDA § 401(c).

41. LMRDA § 401(e).

42. LMRDA § 401(a), (b), (d).

43. LMRDA § 401(c).

44. LMRDA § 401(e).

45. Ibid.

46. LMRDA § 3(k). Secretary of Labor's Regulations, 29 C.F.R. 452.97.

47. Brennan v. Local 3489, Steelworkers, 520 F.2d 516 (7th Cir. 1975). See also Marshall v. Steelworkers Local 12447, 100 LRRM 2383 (3rd Cir. 1978).

48. Goldberg v. Marine Cooks Union, 204 F. Supp. 844 (N.D. Cal. 1962).

49. Compare Hodgson v. Local 920, Teamsters, 327 F. Supp. 1284 (E.D. Tex. 1971) with Hodgson v. Local 582, Plumbers, 350 F. Supp. 16 (C.D. Cal. 1972). See also Secretary of Labor's Regulations, 29 C.F.R. 452.94, .95.

50. See Hodgson v. Local 920, Teamsters, supra note 49, holding this a triable issue of fact.

51. See McDonough v. Local 825, Operating Engineers, 470 F.2d 261 (3rd Cir. 1972), where the specific issue was not reached because the court lacked jurisdiction.

52. Hodgson v. Local 734, Teamsters, 336 F. Supp. 1243 (N.D. Ill. 1972). The court left resolution of this specific issue to trial.

53. Secretary of Labor's Regulations, 29 C.F.R. 452.97 (b), .107.

54. Cf. Hodgson v. Local 920, Teamsters, *supra* note 49.

55. LMRDA § 401(c). The phrase "enforceable at the suit of any bona fide candidate" applies only to the rights listed in the seemingly endless first sentence of 401(c). The rights spelled out in the balance of 401(c) and in the other sections of Title IV do not come under the provision in 401(c) for direct challenge in the courts.

56. *Compare* Sheldon v. O'Callaghan, 335 F. Supp. 325 (S.D. N.Y. 1971), *aff'd.* 497 F.2d 1276 (2nd Cir. 1974), where the court refused to restrain the union from mailing ballots until the challenger could get his materials before the voters, *with* Yablonski v. Mine Workers Union, 305 F. Supp. 868 (D.D.C. 1969), where the court granted preelection relief, observing that the machinery for setting aside an election is "cumbersome, doubtful and calls for delay."

57. LMRDA §§ 401(b), (c), (e), (g).

58. LMRDA § 403.

59. Calhoon v. Harvey, 379 U.S. 134, 140 (1964).

60. LMRDA § 402(a).

61. Cf. Cefalo v. District 50, Mine Workers, 311 F. Supp. 946 (D.D.C. 1970).

62. LMRDA § 402(a).

63. Secretary of Labor's Regulations, 29 C.F.R. 452.136.

64. Trbovich v. Mine Workers Union, 404 U.S. 528 (1972).

65. Hodgson v. Steelworkers Union, 403 U.S. 333 (1971).

66. Wirtz v. Hotel Employees Union, 391 U.S. 492, 505–509 (1968). *See also* Shultz v. Radio Officers Union, *supra* note 32 at 69–70.

67. Shultz v. Radio Officers Union, *supra* note 32 at 64–65.

68. *Ibid.* at 69–70.

69. LMRDA § 402(a).

70. Wirtz v. Local 153, Glass Bottle Blowers Ass'n. 389 U.S. 463 (1968); *compare* Usery v. Masters, Mates

and Pilots Union, 538 F.2d 946 (2nd Cir. 1976) and Marshall v. Teamsters Local 639, 100 LRRM 2487 (D.C. Cir. 1979).

71. LMRDA § 402(c).

72. For critical commentary on the failure of the Secretary of Labor to intervene and for suggestions as to his statutory authority and responsibility to intervene, see Hopson, *The 1969 UMW Election: Why No Pre-Balloting Investigation?* 18 VILL. L. REV. 37 (1972). Good summaries of the full gamut of the litigation arising out of that election are found in Yablonski v. Mine Workers Union, 448 F.2d 1175 (D.C. Cir. 1971) and Yablonski v. Mine Workers Union, 466 F.2d 424 (D.C. Cir. 1972). The chronology of this litigation is set out in Appendix B.

73. See note 72 for a description of the litigation.

74. Yablonski v. Mine Workers Union, 80 LRRM 3435 (D.D.C. 1972).

75. Yablonski v. Mine Workers Union, 448 F.2d 1175 (D.C. Cir. 1971).

76. Blankenship v. Boyle, 329 F.Supp. 296 (D.D.C. 1972); Hodgson v. Mine Workers Union, 344 F. Supp. 990 (D.D.C. 1972).

77. Yablonski v. Mine Workers Union, 466 F.2d 424 (D.C. Cir. 1972).

78. *See, e.g.,* Collins v. IBEW, 418 F.Supp. 50 (W.D. Pa. 1976).

V

Trusteeships and the Relationship between Parent and Local Union

The structure of most labor unions in the United States begins at the lowest level with the local union, which usually represents the employees of a single employer at a particular location. These local unions may in turn be part of an intermediate body, such as a system council or a joint board. At the top of the organizational system is the parent union, either a national or international body. The international, in turn, is generally affiliated with the AFL-CIO.

To the individual worker, the local is the everyday, working face of the union. The local represents him in day-to-day grievance matters and often negotiates his contract. While the individual's dues may be split between the local and international, the individual looks to the local treasury for support of many of the union's activities—for example, in many cases, the payment of the costs of arbitration.

Given the structure of unions, it is understandable that conflicts may arise between the parent and a local. Usually they involve either attempts by the parent to take over the local or by the local to secede from the parent organization. In either case the ultimate issue is one of control: not only of the day-to-day affairs of the local, but of the assets, particularly the treasury, that have accumulated over the years at the local level.

What is a trusteeship and why would one be imposed?

A trusteeship, in general terms, is a takeover by a parent union of one or more of its locals, under which the local loses its autonomy. The parent union may attempt to control the treasury of the local, conduct its affairs, and perhaps even replace its officers.[1] There are valid reasons for a parent to impose a trusteeship. For example, there may be corruption and waste of assets at the local level. Or the local union may be derelict in enforcing its collective-bargaining agreement and the parent may have to step in. On the other hand the parent union may have improper motives: to raid a healthy local treasury or to remove a local officer who has challenged the leadership at the international level.[2]

At common law, the right of a parent union to impose a trusteeship was thought to depend largely upon the terms of the union constitution, although some courts found ways to avoid upholding a trusteeship that appeared to be proper under the union constitution.[3] But the trusteeship device was abused; the McClellan Committee found that three unions in particular had taken advantage of the trusteeship procedure. These abuses included an undue frequency of trusteeships, trusteeships of unreasonably long duration, and improper purposes for creating the trusteeship. This evidence led to the enactment of Title III of the LMRDA, which closely regulates the imposition of trusteeships.[4]

Under what circumstances may a union impose a trusteeship?

Title III of the LMRDA sets forth detailed limitations on imposing a trusteeship. First of all, no trusteeship may be imposed unless the constitution and bylaws of the union provide for it.[5] Courts are reluctant to imply the power to impose trusteeships, and it must be spelled out clearly if it is to be used.[6] Further, the trusteeship must be established in accordance with procedures set out in the constitution and bylaws.[7] Thus, if the constitution requires a notice and hearing before establishing a trusteeship, a trusteeship imposed without this is invalid. And even if there are no procedural requirements in the union constitution and bylaws, the courts have held that a hearing must be held prior to the imposition of a trusteeship.[8]

But compliance with procedural requirements is not enough. Section 302 of the LMRDA closely limits the proper grounds for imposing a trusteeship:

1. Correcting corruption or financial malpractice.
2. Assuring the performance of collective-bargaining agreements or other duties of a bargaining representative.
3. Restoring democratic procedures.
4. Otherwise carrying out the legitimate objects of such labor organization.

There has not been very much case law as to how the above grounds for establishing a trusteeship are satisfied; as would be expected, the last criterion, "otherwise carrying out the legitimate objects of such labor organization," has the greatest potential for litigation because it is the most general of the grounds set forth in Section 302. Further, the Secretary of Labor has indicated some reluctance to prevent the imposition of a trusteeship: "Union trusteeships, although sometimes used to control subordinated organizations illegally, most often are used to provide assistance to subordinates in difficulties, to assist in maintenance and stability, and to promote rather than stifle union democracy." [9]

The difficulty of applying these tests is illustrated by a recent decision that would not allow the parent to impose a trusteeship for the purpose of preventing a district lodge from negotiating a collective-bargaining agreement, where the parent wanted all bargaining to be done on a coordinated basis. [10]

What happens when a trusteeship is imposed?

The parent union will probably take control of the local's treasury and monitor its receipts and expenditures. However, the LMRDA provides that the parent may not siphon funds out of the local and into the parent's treasury except for the normal per-capita tax and assessments normally payable. [11] To achieve this monitoring the parent may impose its own set of officers on the local and manage its day-to-day affairs. It appears that a parent union has this right under Title III, even though its conduct would seem to violate the provisions of Title I and IV dealing with conduct of meetings and election of officers. [12]

The parent union may also attempt to control the local's political influence on the parent—for example, by putting its own representative into office so that he will vote in favor of the parent's interests at a delegate convention. This was a common abuse of the trusteeship, and Congress made clear in Section 303(a)(1) that a parent union may not count the votes of any delegate of a local in trusteeship if that delegate was not chosen fairly in a secret-ballot election.

A trusteeship is presumed valid for eighteen months. After that it must be dissolved unless the union can show "by clear and convincing proof" that a longer period is needed to achieve the purposes permitted under the act.[13]

During the trusteeship, the labor organization must file periodic reports with the Secretary of Labor. These must spell out the purposes of the trusteeship, report on the manner in which the union is carrying out its day-to-day affairs, and contain a complete financial report.[14]

Trusteeships have been infrequent since the enactment of Title III. Statistics show that they declined markedly after the LMRDA became effective.[15]

What may an individual do if he thinks a trusteeship has been imposed or administered improperly?

Title III of the LMRDA permits an individual to file a complaint with the Secretary of Labor. The secretary must investigate, and if he finds probable cause to believe that there is a continuing violation of the trusteeship obligations, he must sue in federal court to terminate these violations. The act provides that the identity of the complaining member is not to be disclosed.[16]

The individual may not have any success with the Secretary of Labor, whose institutional concerns may be different than those of the individual. If the secretary does not file a complaint, the individual may bring his own lawsuit under Title III; he need not first exhaust his administrative remedy with the Secretary of Labor.[17] Nor must he first exhaust his internal remedies within the union; it has been held that the duty to exhaust internal union remedies does not apply in Title III suits.[18]

The Secretary of Labor has broad investigatory powers under Title VI of the LMRDA, and these have been used to investigate trusteeships. The secretary may act under this section even if he has evidence short of probable cause—that is, he may investigate even if he does not know if a violation of the LMRDA has actually occurred.[19]

May a local union withdraw from a parent union?

Unless there is a provision in the union constitution that prohibits disaffiliation, the answer is generally yes; a local union is free to sever its affiliation with the parent.[20]

What happens to the local union's treasury in such a case?

In most cases the local's funds will revert to the parent union. This is because most union constitutions provide for this, and courts generally uphold this result under a contract theory. But some courts have supported the local's retention of funds, particularly where the constitution did not clearly point the other way. For example, in a well-known case in which the parent union was expelled from the AFL-CIO for corruption, the court concluded that the parent had breached its implied promise to the local to remain within the federation, and therefore the local could keep its funds.[21]

What happens to the collective-bargaining relationship if a trusteeship is imposed or the local withdraws from the international?

Generally, the bargaining relationship remains the same. The contract is enforceable by the party named in the agreement, and this is not changed by a disaffiliation or a trusteeship. Of course, if the collective-bargaining agreement names both the local and the international as parties, problems can arise, but these go beyond the scope of this book.

If, as a result of the disaffiliation, the local becomes

defunct, or if the trusteeship fails to correct an inability
of the local to administer the contract properly, the
NLRB's normal contract bars may be abandoned and
a rival union permitted to seek an election. Under the
"contract bar" doctrine, another union normally may
not seek an election while a valid collective bargaining
agreement is in effect. But where the bargaining representative becomes defunct, a distinct possibility under
a trusteeship or disaffiliation, another union is free to
seek a change in bargaining representative.[22]

NOTES

1. A trusteeship is defined in LMRDA § 3(h) as "any
   receivership, trusteeship, or other method of supervision or control whereby a labor organization suspends the autonomy otherwise available to a subordinate body under its constitution or bylaws." For a
   general discussion of trusteeships prior to the
   LMRDA, see Beaird, *Union Trusteeship Provision of
   the LMRDA*, 2 GA. L. REV. 469, 471–474 (1968).
   For a general discussion of the incidence and purposes
   of trusteeships in the early years of the LMRDA, see
   SECRETARY OF LABOR, UNION TRUSTEESHIPS: REPORT
   TO THE CONGRESS UPON THE OPERATION OF TITLE III
   OF THE LMRDA 5–11 (1962), submitted to Congress
   pursuant to Sec. 305 of the LMRDA. See also Ander-
   son, *Landrum-Griffin and the Trusteeship Imbroglio*,
   71 YALE L. J. 1460 (1962).
2. See, e.g., Schonfeld v. Raftery, 271 F. Supp. 128
   (S.D. N.Y. 1967).
3. See Beaird, *Union Trusteeship Provisions of the
   LMRDA*, 2 GA. L. REV. 469, 474–85 (1968).
4. Ibid. at 485–89.
5. LMRDA § 302.
6. Carpenters Union v. Brown, 343 F.2d 872 (10th Cir.
   1965).

7. LMRDA § 302.

8. Local 13410, Mine Workers, 475 F.2d 906 (D.C. Cir. 1973). *See* Note, *A Fair Hearing Requirement for Union Trusteeships under the LMRDA,* 40 U. CHI. L. REV. 873 (1973).

9. SECRETARY OF LABOR, REPORT ON OPERATION OF TITLE III, *supra* note 1.

10. Benda v. Grand Lodge, Machinists Union, 584 F.2d 308 (9th Cir. 1978). *Compare* Carpenters Union v. Brown, 343 F.2d 872 (10 Cir. 1965) (trusteeship improper where purpose is to force local to affiliate with district council and raise its dues) *with* Musicians Local 10 v. Musicians Union, 57 LRRM 2227 (N.D. Ill. 1964) (trusteeship valid where aimed at eliminating racially segregated locals).

11. LMRDA § 303(a)(2).

12. Blassie v. Poole, 58 LRRM 2359 (E.D. Mo. 1965).

13. LMRDA § 304(c).

14. LMRDA § 301.

15. SECRETARY OF LABOR, REPORT ON OPERATION OF TITLE III, *supra* note 1.

16. LMRDA § 304(a).

17. LMRDA § 306.

18. Carpenters Union v. Brown, *supra* note 6.

19. LMRDA § 601. *See, e.g.,* Teamsters v. Wirtz, 346 F.2d 827 (D.C. Cir. 1965).

20. *See generally* Summers, *Union Schism in Perspective,* 45 VA. L. REV. 261 (1959).

21. Crocker v. Weil, 227 Ore. 260, 361 P.2d 1014 (1961). *See* the perceptive opinion of Justice Breitel *in* Bradley v. O'Hare, 11 A.D.2d 15, 202 N.Y.S. 2d 141 (1st Dep't 1960). Summers is critical of those decisions that have manipulated the contractual language of the union constitution to achieve results, usually favorable to the local, in accordance with the court's notion of the propriety of the secession, Summers, *supra* note 20, at 262–69. *See also* Note, *Effect of a Union Split upon Property Rights,* 1952 WISC. L. REV. 139.

22. *See* Summers *supra* note 20. at 269–74. The leading NLRB case on the applicability of contract-bar doctrines in the case of schisms or defunct unions is Hershey Chocolate Corp., 121 NLRB 901 (1958).

VI

Rights in Union Funds and
Fiduciary Obligations
of Union Officers

Does a union member have any rights in the assets of the union?

The question of who owns the union's assets, including its treasury, requires an examination of both the union constitution and bylaws and applicable state law. If the union constitution and bylaws are silent, the union's assets probably belong to the membership, and if the union is dissolved, each member would be entitled to a proportionate share. But in an ongoing union, the constitution and bylaws vest control of the union's assets in its officers. Further, the constitution is likely to provide that upon dissolution of a local its funds revert to the parent union.

But in a broader sense the member does have a recognized right and interest in his union's funds and in the way the union is run. Congress, in imposing certain financial-disclosure requirements upon unions (which will be discussed shortly) observed:

The members of a labor organization are the real owners of the money and property of such organizations and are entitled to a full accounting of all transactions involving such money and property. Because union funds belong to the members they should be expended only in furtherance of their common interest. A union treasury should not be managed as though it were the private property of the union officers, however well intentioned such officers might be, but as a fund governed by fiduciary standards. . . .[1]

This obligation underlies Title V of the LMRDA entitled "Fiduciary Responsibility of Officers of Labor Organizations."

What is a union officer's obligation under Title V?
Title V of the LMRDA imposes a very heavy obligation of trust upon union officers, shop stewards, and others.[2] It states that such persons "occupy positions of trust in relation to such organization and its members as a group." It then imposes specific obligations upon such persons, but subject to a proviso that the fiduciary obligation is to take into account "the special problems and functions of a labor organization." This clause makes clear that the fiduciary standards imposed upon persons in other fields—for example, directors of a corporation—do not necessarily apply in their entirety to officers of a union. The specific obligations imposed upon a union officer under Section 501 include:

1. To hold and expend money and property of the union solely for the benefit of the organization and its members.
2. To refrain from dealing with the union as an adverse party.
3. To avoid any financial or personal interest which conflicts with the interests of the union.

4. To account to the union for any profit received in any transactions conducted on behalf of the organization.

Several important cases have arisen under Section 501, which have circumscribed the powers of union officials. For example, in one case, a divided court held that the officers of the National Maritime Union violated their fiduciary obligation to the membership when they set up a pension plan for certain employees of the union, including the president, who was to receive substantial benefits under the program. The court struck down the plan even though the membership voted overwhelmingly to authorize the program set up by the officers.[3] In another case a court held that an officer violated Section 501 when he allowed his "personal feelings" to influence a decision to require a local union to participate in a pension plan.[4] These decisions have been criticized as going beyond the intended scope of Section 501 and constituting an unwarranted intrusion by the courts into the internal affairs of unions.[5]

In order to safeguard union members, union officials are required under Section 502 of the LMRDA to bond themselves against loss caused by violations of their Title V obligations.

Other statutes also guard against improper use of funds by union officials. For example, Section 302(a) of the Taft-Hartley Law restricts payments by employers to union representatives.[6] It is directed, obviously, at bribery of union officials. The section contains exceptions for legitimate payments by employers to unions—for example, to set up trust funds to provide health insurance for bargaining-unit employees.[7]

How can a member find out whether union officers are properly handling union funds and managing its affairs?

Every labor union is required to file detailed annual reports with the Secretary of Labor.[8] These reports must contain a full statement of the assets and liabilities of the organization, the sources of revenue, the names of officers and employees who receive more than $10,000 per year from the union, loans to employees or members in excess of $250, and other loans and disbursements made by the union. The reports must be filed for local as well as intermediate and parent bodies.

This information must be made available to all members of the union; in addition, the reports are public and may be examined by anyone, even a non-member of the union.

These reports are required to disclose a variety of information other than financial data. For example, the union is required to disclose the dues and initiation fees, and to identify its rules and regulations for dealing with internal matters, such as levying assessments and for disciplining or removing officers or agents of the union.

May a member recover legal costs if he is forced to sue the union to obtain this information or to secure compliance with the officers' fiduciary duties?

Yes. The statute provides for the court to award attorney's fees and costs, in its discretion, where a member prevails in a lawsuit requiring the union to disclose material that should have been made available under Title II.[9] The theory behind this is that the individual who sues the union in such a case performs a service to the union as well as to himself; since the union benefits from the lawsuit it ought to pay for it. The same provision is made for counsel fees where an individual succeeds in a Title V suit against an officer for breach of his fiduciary responsibility.[10]

May an officer use union funds or the services of union counsel to defend himself in a lawsuit in which he is charged with abuse of his responsibilities under Title V?

No. The courts have made clear that a union officer charged with a breach of his fiduciary duties under Title V may not use union funds or union counsel to defend himself. As one court put it:

> To allow a union officer to use the power and wealth of the very union which he is accused of pilfering, to defend himself against such charges, is totally inconsistent with Congress's effort to eliminate the undesirable element which has been uncovered in the labor-management field. To allow even a majority of members in that union to authorize such action, when, if the charges made against these defendants are true, it is these very members whom the officers have deceived, would be equally inconsistent with the Act.[11]

Of course there may be cases in which the lawsuit is plainly a frivolous one, or may have "a direct and injurious effect upon the union." In such a case the court may use its discretion under Section 502(b) of the LMRDA to throw the lawsuit out if it appears to be frivolous; or the court may permit the union to finance the defense of the lawsuit. And if the union officer who finances his own defense succeeds in establishing that he has done no wrong, the union may be allowed to reimburse him for the expenses he incurred in defending the lawsuit.[12]

What other safeguards are there against the abuse of power by union officers?

Section 601 of the LMRDA gives the Secretary of

Labor the power, "when he believes it necessary in order to determine whether any person has violated or is about to violate any provision of this Act" (except for Title I), to make necessary investigations. This power includes the right to enter places, subpoena documents, and inspect records. The weapon is a potent one, for the secretary need not establish probable cause to begin an investigation under Title VI.[13] (In contrast, under Title III, he may seek judicial relief against a trusteeship only if he has probable cause to believe that Title III has been violated.) The secretary's investigative powers under Title VI have been used with some success to expose instances of corruption. But, as with all claims that rely upon the Secretary of Labor for action, the individual worker cannot be sure that the secretary will view the problem in the same perspective or accord it the same priority as he does.

Recent cases hold that the fiduciary obligations imposed upon union officers under Title V of the LMRDA extend to all the functions of officers, not only those related to union funds.[14]

NOTES

1. H.R. REP. No. 741 ON H.R. 8342. 86th Cong, 1st Sess. 7–9 (1959).
2. LMRDA § 501(a). For a comprehensive discussion of the scope of Title V, *see* Note, *Counsel Fees for Union Officers under the Fiduciary Provision of Landrum-Griffin*, 73 YALE L. J. 443 (1964); *see also* Clark, *The Fiduciary Duties of Union Officials under Section 501 of the LMRDA*, 52 MINN. L. REV. 437 (1967).
3. Morrissey v. Curran, 423 F.2d 393 (2nd Cir. 1970), *cert. denied*, 399 U.S. 928, 400 U.S. 826 (1970).

4. Pignotti v. Local #3, Sheet Metal Workers, 477 F.2d 825 (8th Cir. 1978), *cert. denied,* 414 U.S. 1067 (1973).
5. Leslie, *Federal Courts and Union Fiduciaries,* 76 COLUM. L. REV. 1314 (1976); *see also* Gabauer v. Woodcock, 97 LRRM 2698 (8th Cir. 1978).
6. NLRA § 302(a).
7. The exceptions are set forth in NLRA § 302(c).
8. The reporting requirements are contained in LMRDA Title II; *see* §§ 201, 202. For an amplification of these rights *see* Local 1419 Longshore Workers v. Smith, 301 F.2d 791 (5th Cir. 1962). Additional reporting requirements are imposed in the case of pension funds under the Employee Retirement Income Security Act of 1974 (ERISA).
9. LMRDA § 201(c).
10. LMRDA § 501(b). *Compare* Yablonski v. Mine Workers Union, 448 F.2d 1175 (D.C. Cir. 1971), *cert. denied,* 406 U.S. 906 (1971) *and* Bakery Workers Union v. Ralner, 118 U.S. App. D.C. 269, 335 F.2d 691 (D.C. Cir. 1964).
11. Highway Truck Drivers Local 107 v. Cohen, 182 F. Supp. 608 (E.D. Pa. 1960).
12. *See, generally,* Note, *Counsel Fees, supra,* note 2, at 443, 454–67.
13. Teamsters Union v. Wirtz, 346 F.2d 827 (D.C. Cir. 1965).
14. Stelling v. IBEW Local 1547, 100 LRRM 2366 (9th Cir. 1978); *see comment,* The Fiduciary Duty under Section 501 of the LMRDA, 75 COLUM. L. REV. 1189 (1975).

VII

The Duty of Fair Representation

A distinctive feature of our system of labor relations is that a single union, the union selected by the majority of the employees in the bargaining unit, is authorized to speak and act on behalf of all employees in the bargaining unit, regardless of whether they are union members or want to be represented by the union. This authority, which is expressly granted to unions under our labor statutes, is known as the rule of exclusive representation.[1] As a result, the individual employee has no independent right to set his own terms of employment or to enforce his rights under a collective-bargaining agreement.[2] Nor can he turn to another union to protect his rights if he is dissatisfied with the way negotiations are proceeding or the contract is being enforced.[3]

The courts have held that the vast statutory authority a union has by virtue of its status as exclusive bargaining representative requires that it represent fairly all employees in the bargaining unit. The courts have likened this responsibility to the obligation a legislature owes to its electorate or a trustee owes to those he represents.[4] This duty of fair representation was first applied by the courts in cases in which the union had discriminated against employees on the basis of race. But the duty of fair representation now goes much further and reaches any form of discrimination or unfair treatment of any employees in the bargaining unit. It encompasses the negotiation of the collective-bargaining agreement, the processing of a grievance, including the decision whether to press a grievance to arbitration, and the presentation of the grievance in arbitration. The duty of fair representation is not easy to describe, for it depends upon the facts of each case and involves a delicate balancing of individual interests with the needs of the larger group.[5]

How is the duty of fair representation defined?

The Supreme Court has provided some general guidelines that help define the duty of fair representation. In one of the earliest cases, *Steele* v. *Louisville RR.*,[6] involving a charge that a railroad union had discriminated against black employees whom it represented, the Court held that the statutory bargaining agent must exercise its power on behalf of all employees in the bargaining unit "without hostile discrimination, fairly, impartially and in good faith." [7] Under this test it was quite clear that the union could not negotiate different benefits for different groups of employees on the basis of their race.

More than twenty years later, in the landmark case of *Vaca* v. *Sipes,* the Supreme Court elaborated upon the duty of fair representation.[8] An employee who had been discharged because of poor health claimed that the union had improperly refused to take his case to arbitration. While the Court held that an individual has no absolute right to have his grievance taken to arbitration, the language of the decision expanded the union's obligation of fair representation in processing grievances. The Court held that in addition to its obligation to process the grievance in good faith and without discrimination, the union "may not arbitrarily ignore a meritorious grievance or process it in a perfunctory fashion." [9] In subsequent cases the lower courts have tended to concentrate on the portion of the *Vaca* test prohibiting "arbitrary" conduct by the union;[10] some courts have also applied the language condemning "perfunctory" handling of a grievance, although, as we shall see, courts have been reluctant to find a breach of fair representation under this test unless the union's carelessness is quite extreme.[11]

The standards for fair representation in negotiating an agreement may be different from those in processing a grievance. The following questions and answers provide more concrete examples of the union's duty of fair representation in each context.

What is the union's duty of fair representation in negotiating an agreement?

The union has considerable leeway in negotiating an agreement that advances the overall concerns of the bargaining unit at the expense of some individuals and groups within the unit. For example, a union negotiated a provision in a collective-bargaining agreement that gave employees seniority credit for service in the armed forces. This gave employees who were hired after completion of military service greater seniority than some employees who were hired earlier, but who had not served in the armed forces. In upholding the union's right to negotiate this type of seniority arrangement, the Supreme Court stated:

A major responsibility of negotiators is to weigh the relative advantages and disadvantages of differing proposals. . . . The complete satisfaction of all who are represented is hardly to be expected. A wide range of reasonableness must be allowed a statutory bargaining representative in serving the unit it represents, subject always to complete good faith and honesty of purpose in the exercise of its discretion.[12]

Under this principle, a union might decide that more employees would be benefited by a substantial wage increase than by a pension program that would divert some of the wage increase. While some employees, particularly those nearer retirement, might prefer a pension program to a large wage increase, their only recourse is to the democratic political process within the union. That is, they can try to influence the bargaining committee to obtain a pension program, but they cannot compel them to do so under the duty of fair representation.

Many of the challenges to the terms of an agreement negotiated by the union involve seniority questions arising out of mergers and other reorganizations of employers. For example, if one trucking company absorbs another, the union must decide how to merge the seniority lists of the two employers. It might "dovetail" the seniority lists, crediting each employee with his full seniority with his respective company, or it might "endtail" the employees of the absorbed company, placing all of them below the employees of the other company on the seniority lists. Under either arrangement, or some variation in between, some employees are likely to be dissatisfied. For, as one commentator has observed, "on seniority issues the union's position cannot logically be neutral; it must, of necessity, support the views of one individual or group against those of another." [13] The union's determination will usually be upheld if supported on some rational basis, particularly if the union has carefully investigated the merits of the conflicting seniority interests.

However, recent cases suggest the courts will scrutinize more carefully the basis for a union's determination as to seniority. In one case, a larger company bought a smaller one at a time when expansion was anticipated. The union and the employer agreed to dovetail the seniority of the employees at the two locations. The business later slowed down and the employees who had been with the larger company feared that the employees of the smaller company might displace them under the dovetailing system if there were a reduction in jobs. When the collective bargaining agreement expired, the employees of the larger company persuaded the union and the company to negotiate an endtail seniority system, which would protect the seniority rights of the employees of the larger company. The court held that this was a breach of the duty of fair representation: "Such decisions may not be made solely for the benefit of a stronger, more politically favored group, over a minority group." [14] These recent decisions cast in doubt an earlier, well-known case that upheld a seniority determination made on a political basis,[15] but that has been sharply criticized in the literature.[16]

A negotiated agreement reached in bad faith or on an arbitrary or discriminatory basis will not stand. For example, as the Supreme Court held in *Steele*,[17] a union may not negotiate different lines of promotion for different groups on the basis of race. Nor may it ignore existing contractual guidelines covering merger situations.[18] In a recent case it was alleged that a union negotiated an area wage agreement for truckdrivers that was below the wage level that had been agreed upon nationally. The union concealed this fact from the membership and refused to allow the members to vote on the wage agreement. The members contended that had they known the facts and been given an opportunity to vote, they would have rejected the settlement. The court held that these facts, if proved, would establish arbitrary, discriminatory, or bad-faith conduct by the union in negotiations.[19]

What is the union's duty of fair representation in processing an individual's grievance?

The union's obligation of fair representation in processing a grievance is basically twofold:

1. It must process the grievance with some degree of care, make an appropriate investigation of the facts, and observe contractual time limits.
2. After making this investigation, the union must decide whether to pursue the grievance further, especially whether to take the grievance to arbitration. This determination must not be arbitrary, discriminatory, or in bad faith.

Many recent cases involve claims of carelessness in investigating and processing the grievance. For, as one commentator has observed, "the individual's interest may more often be vitiated without vindictiveness or deliberate discrimination. Incomplete investigation of the facts, reliance on untested evidence, or colored evaluation of witnesses may lead the union to reject grievances which more objective inquiry would prove meritorious." [20] Thus, a union may not wholly ignore a grievance, refuse to make a thorough investigation, or fail to follow up leads suggested by the grievant. All of this falls into the category of arbitrary or perfunctory treatment.[21]

In one case, an employee, Griffin, was disciplined for reading a newspaper on the job and was later fired when he got into a fight at a hockey game with the supervisor who had disciplined him earlier. Griffin grieved his discharge, which was filed by the union grievance chairman with the same supervisor who had fought with Griffin. The supervisor refused to reinstate Griffin, and the union dropped the grievance for a lengthy period, finally agreeing to revive it. Griffin sued the union for breach of fair representation in its manner of handling the grievance. The court agreed with him on several grounds, one of which was the decision of the grievance chairman to file the grievance with the supervisor involved in the fight. The court said:

> The union's insistence on filing the discharge grievance with . . . the man whom Griffin had fought, cannot be justified. It represents a stubborn refusal to recognize the inequity of placing the matter in the hands of a hostile person— Griffin's antagonist. Although the union may have acted in good faith, grieving the discharge in this manner can be viewed . . . as the equivalent of arbitrarily ignoring the grievance or handling it in a perfunctory manner.[22]

In another case, the union misplaced a grievance submitted to it and allowed the contractual time limits for filing grievances to pass. The court held this to be a breach of the duty of fair representation: "When a union makes no decision as to the merit of an individual's grievance but merely allows it to expire by failing to take a basic and required step toward resolving it, the union has acted arbitrarily and is liable for a breach of the duty of fair representation." [23]

In one recent case, an airline clerk was discharged because of a medical condition that led to excessive absenteeism and poor work. She grieved the discharge, and was offered a settlement by the employer, which would have reinstated her without back pay on a probationary basis and with an impairment of seniority. She refused the settlement and was discharged. The grievant alleged that when she turned down the settlement she was not aware that the union had no intention of taking her case to arbitration. Had she known that the case would not be taken to arbitration, she contended, she would have accepted the settlement. The court agreed that if the case went to trial the facts might show a breach of the duty of fair representation on the ground that the union's conduct was "so egregious, so far short of minimum standards of fairness to the employee and so unrelated to legitimate union interests as to be arbitrary." [24]

It has been suggested that recent cases, such as some of the ones discussed in this question, represent an expansion of the category of "arbitrary" and "perfunctory" treatment, condemned by the court in *Vaca*.[25] One commentator, whose practice includes the representation of unions, has observed,

A nonhostile and nondiscriminatory evaluation by the union that the employer would probably be successful at arbitration, because the facts known at the time of the grievance procedure were more supportive of the employer's position than of the employees', no longer constitutes an adequate defense where the union should have conducted a more thorough and complete investigation of the facts with which it would then confront the employer during the grievance procedure. . . .

As to the expanded union obligation, I depart from the good-faith views asserted by some of my colleagues who represent unions; instead I share the view that increasing the standards by which a labor organization is to be judged in the long run will strengthen the democratic fabric which we assert is an outstanding quality of the American labor movement.[26]

If an individual is not satisfied with the way the union is processing her grievance, she may take it up with the employer on her own. However, the union must be given an opportunity to be present at the discussion of the grievance. The union can object if the settlement is inconsistent with the collective-bargaining agreement.[27] As a practical matter, if the union opposes the settlement, it is not likely that the individual will achieve a favorable result.

The second aspect of the union's duty to process a grievance involves its decision whether to take the grievance to the next step. This question usually arises at the arbitration stage, although it can come up at an earlier point in the grievance process. This aspect of the union's obligation of fair representation is discussed in connection with the next question.

What is the union's obligation to take a grievance to arbitration?

Under most collective-bargaining agreements, the union controls access to arbitration. For example, a typical clause provides:

ARTICLE XIV: GRIEVANCES AND ARBITRATION
A. For the purpose of this agreement, a "grievance" is a dispute between the Company and the Union concerning the interpretation or application of a specific provision of this Agreement.

The Supreme Court's landmark decision of *Vaca* v. *Sipes* made clear that where the collective-bargaining agreement gives the union control over the arbitration process, the individual has no absolute right to take his case to arbitration unless the union consents. The Court said:

> Though we accept the proposition that a union may not arbitrarily ignore a meritorious grievance or process it in perfunctory fashion, we do not agree that the individual employee has an absolute right to have his grievance taken to arbitration. . . . In providing for a grievance and arbitration procedure which gives the union discretion to supervise the grievance machinery and to invoke arbitration, the employer and union contemplate that each will endeavor in good faith to settle grievances short of arbitration. Through this settlement process, frivolous grievances are ended prior to the most costly and time-consuming step in the grievance procedures. Moreover, both sides are assured that similar complaints will be treated consistently, and major problem areas in the interpretation of the collective bargaining contract can be isolated and perhaps resolved.[28]

The Court's ruling in *Vaca* can be better understood by looking at the facts involved. The grievant, Owens, had been out of work on a sick leave, recovering from high blood pressure. When he sought to return to work, the company doctor concluded that his blood pressure was too high for him to resume the heavy work required of him. However, Owens saw two other doctors, who thought he was fit for work. In the course of processing the grievance through the fourth step of the grievance procedure, the union sent Owens to still another doctor, at union expense, to obtain more favorable medical evidence, but the examination did not support the grievant. The union also tried to get Owens a less strenuous job at the plant and "joined in the employer's efforts to have Owens rehabilitated." When all of these approaches failed, the union's executive board voted not to take Owens's grievance to arbitration. Under these circumstances, the Court concluded that the union did not breach its duty of fair representation in refusing to take Owens's case to arbitration. The Court said:

> A union must, in good faith and in a nonarbitrary manner, make decisions as to the merits of particular grievances. . . . In a case such as this, when Owens supplied the union with medical evidence supporting his position, the Union might well have breached its duty had it ignored Owens' complaint or had it processed the grievance in a perfunctory manner. . . . There was no evidence that any Union officer was personally hostile to Owens or that the Union acted at any time other than in good faith.[29]

What factors will determine whether a union breaches its duty of fair representation in refusing to take a case to arbitration?

As indicated in the introduction to this chapter, it is difficult to identify the precise factors that will lead a court to conclude in one case that a union has breached its duty of fair representation and in another case that it has not. The following tests, which are only generalizations, may be helpful:[30]

1. Did the union approach the grievance with an open mind in an honest effort to achieve a fair result? If not—for example, if the union was merely looking for some excuse to drop the case—it violates its duty of fair representation. Thus, a union may not refuse to

take a grievance further because it is hostile to the grievant, perhaps because the grievant has opposed the union leadership in the past.

2. Did the union investigate the case with care and pursue all reasonable evidence suggested by the grievant? If not, a court is likely to find its conduct arbitrary and a breach of the duty of fair representation. While this point was discussed earlier as part of the union's obligation to process the grievance fairly, it also has a bearing upon the union's decision not to take the case further. For example, in a well-known case, some truck drivers were discharged for allegedly padding their receipts for motel expenses. A joint area committee, consisting of employer and union representatives, sustained the discharge. The grievants, who insisted they had not padded the receipts, demanded that the union investigate the motel records, for they believed the motel clerk had falsified the records. The union refused to make this investigation and refused to reopen the case. When it turned out that the motel clerk had in fact altered the motel's records, the court held that the union breached its duty of fair representation in failing to investigate the case properly.[31]

In another case, a union filed a grievance on behalf of a teacher who claimed he was entitled, on the basis of his seniority, to be a department head. When the union won the case in arbitration, the less senior employee who lost the position to the senior teacher claimed that the union had breached its obligation of fair representation to him. The court agreed, holding that where a union decides to choose between competing employees it must at least investigate the claims of all the employees who seek the position, before deciding whose case it will advance to arbitration.[32]

3. Has the union treated the grievance in the same way it has dealt with similar grievances in the past? If

the individual can show that the union has taken similar cases to arbitration, but now refuses to take this one, a breach of the duty of fair representation may be shown.

4. Is the union's decision not to take the case to arbitration consistent with a reasonable interpretation of the contract? The union may properly decide not to pursue the case because it concludes that there is not a good chance that its position will be sustained in arbitration. If the union reaches this conclusion in good faith, it satisfies its duty of fair representation even if it was mistaken about the merits of the case. Thus, a union was upheld in a recent case in which it decided not to pursue a claim by a male employee that a dress requirement that he wear a tie was invalid under the contract. The court held that the union's judgment that the grievance was a "bad case" was not arbitrary.[33] The union's position will be particularly strong if it can point to considerations of time and costs in not pursuing a doubtful case.[34] But where the individual's grievance is a strong one on the merits, and there is little doubt that it would prevail in arbitration, the union may violate its obligation to the employee if it refuses to arbitrate the case.

Does a union violate the duty of fair representation when it trades off grievances?

Sometimes a union and employer to agree to settle a batch of pending grievances by trading them off. Given the costs of arbitration, it may make sense for the union to surrender some grievances of questionable merit in order to gain a favorable settlement in others. It has been urged that wholesale trading off of grievances may violate the duty of fair representation, but the few reported cases on this question are not conclusive. Of course if the union trades off grievances without investigating their merits, or trades off grievances that it believes have a good chance of being won in arbitration, it will have difficulty in arguing that it has fairly represented the grievant. But if the union, after investigation and fair consideration, concludes that certain grievances have little chance of being won in arbitration, it probably does not violate its obligation if it settles them in exchange for meritorious grievances.[35]

Must the union comply with any particular procedural steps before deciding not to take a grievance to arbitration?

Not necessarily. However, if the union provides by constitution, bylaws, or custom for a procedure to review cases before deciding whether to submit them to arbitration, the union must of course follow these procedures. Even if such procedures are not required, the union's decision is more likely to be upheld by the courts if it results from a careful, impartial review, perhaps by vote of the local membership, rather than by the decision of a single official within the union. Some unions provide internal review procedures to insure that these decisions are made fairly.[36]

Does the duty of fair representation apply to the union's presentation of a case in arbitration?

Yes. It is clear that the union's duty of fair representation includes fair representation of the individual in the arbitration hearing.[37] However, the courts give the union a great deal of freedom in deciding how to present the case. Just because the union does a poor job in presenting the case does not necessarily mean that it has breached its duty of fair representation. More is required, such as a showing of arbitrary or bad faith handling of the case, or extremely inadequate preparation and presentation. For example, if the union meets only briefly or not at all with the grievant prior to the case, and as a result omits important evidence, a failure of fair representation may be shown.[38] It is, however, a difficult matter to convince a reviewing court that a fair arbitration was not held, particularly where there is no transcript for the court to review.[39]

May an individual have her own attorney or representative at an arbitration hearing? May she present her own case?

Generally not, for the union usually asserts sole responsibility and authority for presenting the grievance. If the union objects to having a grievance presented by the individual or her representative, the arbitrator will generally not permit it. Whether the individual's representative may be present in the hearing room, and whether the individual may add her own evidence and arguments at the end of the union's presentation, is unsettled.[40]

In some cases the union may agree to let the individual, either by herself or through her representative, present her own case. In effect, the union designates the individual as the union's spokesman. The employer has no basis to oppose the union's choice of spokesperson.[41]

In any event, unless the union and employer consent, the individual may not participate in the selection of the arbitrator. This is done by the union and employer or by an impartial agency like the American Arbitration Association or Federal Mediation and Conciliation Service.

How does an individual make a claim of unfair representation?

The individual can file a charge with the NLRB within six months of the claimed violation.[42] Alternatively, the individual may bring a lawsuit under Section 301 of the LMRA. In this suit the individual will claim both that the employer violated the collective bargaining agreement in its treatment of the individual and that the union breached its duty of fair representation in its handling of the grievance. If the court concludes that the union breached its duty of fair representation, it has the authority to decide the individual's contract claim, or may direct the parties to arbitrate the grievance. The court may apportion damages between the union and the employer. The court may not avoid punitive damages.[43] But if the court concludes that the union did not breach its duty of fair representation in refusing to take a grievance to arbitration, the individual has no further right to have his contract claim arbitrated; the grievance is, for all practical purposes, at an end.[44]

If the individual successfully challenges the union's conduct in a case in which an arbitration was actually held, the court will set the arbitration award aside. It may then decide the grievance itself or order a new arbitration. This is an exception to the general rule that an arbitration award will rarely be set aside by the courts.[45]

Do unions in the public sector owe a duty of fair representation to the employees they represent?

Yes. Cases in the public sector make it increasingly clear that the duty of fair representation applies to public-sector employees as well. The requirements of fair representation may be even more stringent in the public sector because of the constitutional obligations of due process in public employment.[46]

NOTES

1. NLRA § 9(a); RLA § 2, Fourth; and Order of R.R. Telegraphers v. Railway Express Agency, 321 U.S. 342 (1944).
2. J. I. Case Co. v. NLRB, 321 U.S. 332 (1944); Order of R.R. Telegraphers v. Railway Express Agency, *supra* note 1.
3. The NLRA provides a mechanism for employees to change bargaining representatives, but as a practical matter this right is quite limited. For example, if a union is already representing employees and a collective bargaining agreement is in effect, that agreement will bar a representation claim by a rival union except between the sixtieth and ninetieth days prior to the expiration of that agreement. The rules are complicated, *see* GORMAN, BASIC TEXT ON LABOR LAW 54–59 (1976).
4. Tunstall v. Brotherhood of Locomotive Firemen, 323 U.S. 210 (1944).
5. The literature on this subject is vast, and constantly expanding. For a collection of papers exploring a variety of aspects of the problem see JEAN MCKELVEY (ed.), THE DUTY OF FAIR REPRESENTATION (New York State School of Industrial and Labor Relations, Cornell University, 1977) (articles by Aaron, Jones, Vladeck, Lipsitz, Summers, Rabin, Klein, and Donahue). A number of major articles are cited in Koretz and Rabin, *Arbitration and Individual Rights*, in THE FUTURE OF LABOR ARBITRATION IN AMERICA 113, n. 2 (American Arbitration Association, 1976). The most recent of these include Clark, *The Duty of Fair Representation: A Theoretical Structure*, 51 TEXAS L. REV. 1119 (1973); Bryson, *A Matter of Wooden Logic: Labor Law Preemption and Individual Rights*, 51 TEXAS L. REV. 1037 (1973); Tobias, *A Plea for the Wrongfully Discharged Employee Abandoned by His Union*, 41 U. CIN. L. REV. 55 (1972). Two of the earlier classic articles are COX, *The Duty of Fair*

Representation, 2 VILL. L. REV. 151 (1957) *and* Feller, *A General Theory of the Collective Bargaining Agreement*, 61 CALIF. L. REV. 663 (1973).

6. 323 U.S. 192 (1944).

7. *Ibid.* at 204.

8. 386 U.S. 171 (1967).

9. *Ibid.* at 191.

10. Some representative examples include Figueroa v. Packinghouse Workers Union, 425 F.2d 281 (1st Cir. 1970); Griffin v. Auto Workers Union, 469 F.2d 181 (4th Cir. 1972), *and* Morton v. Anchor Motor Freight, 90 LRRM 2427 (S.D. N.Y. 1975).

11. *Compare* Ruzicka v. General Motors, 523 F.2d 306 (7th Cir. 1975) *and* Hines v. Anchor Motor Freight, 424 U.S. 554 (1976) *with* Bazarte v. Transportation Union, 429 F.2d 868 (3rd Cir. 1970) and Teamsters Local 692, 209 NLRB 446, 85 LRRM 1385 (1974). For an inventory of representative cases on arbitrary and perfunctory treatment as of early 1976, *see* Koretz and Rabin, *Arbitration and Individual Rights*, in THE FUTURE OF LABOR ARBITRATION IN AMERICA 113, 126–28 n. 67 (American Arbitration Association, 1976).

12. Ford Motor Co. v. Huffman, 345 U.S. 330, 338 1952). But compare Letter Carriers, Branch 6000 v. NLRB, 100 LRRM 2346 (C.A.D.C. 1979), suggesting that under some circumstances if an agreement is submitted to a referendum vote, non-union members cannot be excluded from that vote.

13. Aaron, *The Duty of Fair Representation: An Overview*, in MCKELVEY, *supra* note 5, at 23.

14. Barton Brands v. NLRB, 529 F.2d 793, 798–99 (7th Cir. 1976); *see also* NLRB v. Teamsters Local 315, 545 F.2d 1173 (9th Cir. 1976).

15. Britt v. Trailmobile Co., 179 F.2d 569 (6th Cir. 1950). Related litigation is found in Trailmobile v. Whirls, 331 U.S. 40 (1947).

16. Summers, *Union Powers and Workers' Rights*, 49 MICH L. REV. 805 (1951).

17. Steele v. Louisville R.R., *supra* note 6.

18. Bieski v. Eastern Automobile Forwarding Co., 396 F.2d 32 (3rd Cir. 1968).
19. Trail v. Teamsters, 542 F.2d 961 (6th Cir. 1976).
20. Summers, *Individual Rights in Collective Agreements and Arbitration,* 37 N.Y.U. L. J. 362, 393 (1962).
21. Hines v. Anchor Motor Freight, *supra,* note 11.
22. Griffin v. Auto Workers Union, *supra* note 10, at 181, 184 (4th Cir. 1972).
23. Ruzicka v. General Motors, *supra* note 11, at 306, 310 (7th Cir. 1975).
24. Robesky v. Qantas Airways, 573 F.2d 1082 (9th Cir. 1978).
25. See Aaron, *supra* note 13, at 8, 18–22. For cases that do not find a breach of the duty of fair representation in careless grievance handling, *see* Bazarte v. Transportation Union, *supra* note 11; Teamsters Local 692, *supra* note 11; *and* Dente v. Masters, Mates and Pilots Union, 492 F.2d 10 (9th Cir. 1974).
26. Lipsitz, *The Implication of Hines v. Anchor Motor Freight, in* McKelvey, *supra* note 5, at 55, 58.
27. NLRA § 9(a).
28. Vaca v. Sipes, *supra* note 8, at 191.
29. *Ibid.* at 194.
30. Further examples of factors that may determine whether a union breaches its duty of fair representation may be found in seven sample cases presented in Summers, *The Individual Employee's Rights Under the Collective Agreement: What Constitutes Fair Representation?* 126 U. Pa. L. Rev. 251, 263–78 (1977).
31. Hines v. Anchor Motor Freight, *supra* note. 11.
32. Belanger v. Matteson, 346 A.2d 124 (R.I. S. Ct. 1975). *Compare* Smith v. Hussman Refrigerator Co., 100 LRRM 2338 (8th Cir. 1979).
33. Fountain v. Safeway Stores, 555 F.2d 753 (9th Cir. 1977).
34. Curth v. Faraday, 401 F.Supp. 678 (E.D. Mich. 1975).
35. This question is discussed in Summers, *supra* n. 30, at 270–72. *See* Harrison v. United Transportation

Union, 530 F.2d 558 (4th Cir. 1975), *cert. denied,* 425 U.S. 958 (1976), *and* Local 13, ILWU v. Pacific Maritime Association, 441 F.2d 1061 (9th Cir. 1971), *cert. denied,* 404 U.S. 1016 (1971).

36. *See* Klein, *Enforcement of the Right to Fair Representation: Alternative Forums,* in MCKELVEY, *supra* note 5, at 97.

37. Hines v. Anchor Motor Freight, *supra* note 11.

38. Holodnak v. Avco Corp. 381 F.Supp. 191 (D. Conn. 1974), *aff'd in part and rev'd in part,* 514 F.2d 285 (2nd Cir. 1975).

39. For a more detailed discussion of the question of adequacy of representation in arbitration and of some representative cases, *see* Rabin, *The Duty of Fair Representation in Arbitration,* in MCKELVEY, *supra* note 5, at 84. *Compare* Bantley v. Lucky Stores, 95 LRRM 3232 (N.D. Cal. 1977) with Allsbrook v. Consol. Freightways, 96 LRRM 2628 (E.D. Pa. 1977).

40. *See* Russell v. Patterson, 55 A.D.2d 619, 389 N.Y.S. 2d 411 (2nd Dep't 1976); Teamsters Local 396, 220 NLRB 35 (1975), *enf'd,* 509 F.2d 1075 (9th Cir. 1975); Laney v. Ford Motor Co., 95 LRRM 2003 (D. Minn. 1977).

41. For the procedural problems this may create, *see* Hotel Employees v. Michaelson's, 545 F.2d 1248 (9th Cir. 1976), and the arbitrator's interim award at 61 LA 1195.

42. NLRA §§ 8(b)(1)(A) and 10(b).

43. Electrical Workers v. Foust, —— U.S. ——, 101 LRRM 2365 (Sup. Ct. 1979).

44. Vaca v. Sipes, *supra* note 8; Republic Steel Corp v. Maddox, 379 U.S. 650 (1965).

45. See Note, *Employee Challenges to Arbitral Awards,* 125 U. PA. L. REV. 1310 (1977).

46. *See, e.g.,* Belanger v. Matteson, *supra* note 32; Jackson v. Regional Transit Service, 54 A.D.2d 305, 388 N.Y.S.2d 441 (4th Dept. 1976). *See* Aaron *supra* note 13, at 8, 16–18.

VIII

The Right Not to Be a Union Member

A volatile political and philosophical issue in labor law is whether an employee may be required to join a union in order to obtain or keep his job. Unions desire some form of compulsory union membership because bargaining strength is enhanced if the union does not have to devote its energies to membership drives and does not have to worry about membership defections and maintaining majority status. Historically, unions have also used union-security provisions to give their members priority in obtaining jobs. And since the union has a duty to negotiate and administer a contract on behalf of all persons in the bargaining unit, it has a legitimate claim on each person in the bargaining unit to pay his fair share of the expenses of collective bargaining. But in a society with a deep commitment to individual rights, there are strong arguments against requiring an individual to join a union. The individual may be philosophically opposed to unions or unwilling to submit to certain union rules and regulations that would affect his conduct.

Congress and the courts have reached a compromise

on the question of compulsory union membership. As explained in detail in the following questions and answers, a union may not compel an employee to assume full union membership as a condition of holding a job. But the union may require the individual to pay regular dues and initiation fees in order to defray the costs of union representation. While this arrangement may take several forms, we refer generally in this chapter to such a requirement as a "union-security" provision.

The question of compulsory union membership is governed primarily by the National Labor Relations Act (NLRA), particularly Section 7, which provides: "Employees . . . shall also have the right to refrain from any or all activities except to the extent that such right may be affected by an agreement requiring membership in a labor organization as a condition of employment as authorized in Section 8(a)(3)." The latter section sets out the ground rules for union-security agreements. The Railway Labor Act contains similar provisions covering employees in the transportation industries. In addition, in those industries covered by the NLRA, states have the authority under Section 14(b) to prohibit union-security agreements. The relevant statutory provisions are found in Appendix A.

Can a union require that the employer hire only union members?

No. The statute does not allow a union-security arrangement that gives preference in hiring to union members or requires that a person already be a member of the union as a condition of being hired. Such an arrangement, known as a closed-shop agreement, was outlawed by Congress in the 1947 Taft-Hartley amendments. The obligations under a union-security clause may not be imposed upon an employee until thirty days after the beginning of his employment.[1]

How does a union-security provision operate?

A union-security clause is a provision in a collective-bargaining agreement under which an employee is required to pay for the basic financial costs of representation by the union in order to keep his job.[2] A vote by the employees in the bargaining unit is not required before such a provision may be incorporated in the agreement, but there is a procedure under the NLRA for employees to vote to remove a union-security provision from an agreement.[3] Unless a union-security agreement is contained in the collective-bargaining agreement, an employee is under no readily enforceable obligation to pay for the costs of union representation.

Is an employee obliged to join the union under a union-security clause?

No. An employee cannot be forced, under a union-security clause, to assume the full obligations of union membership. In a major decision on this point, the Supreme Court observed that under the second proviso to Section 8(a)(3) of the NLRA, the employer may discharge an employee under a union-security clause only if the employee fails to tender—that is, to offer to pay—periodic dues and initiation fees. This provision does not permit or oblige the employer to discharge an employee because he has refused to join the union. Thus, the Supreme Court said, " 'Membership' as a condition of employment is whittled down to its financial core." [4] Of course, if the employee voluntarily joins the union he assumes all the membership obligations spelled out in the union constitution and bylaws. But even where the employee voluntarily assumes full membership, he may be discharged from his employment only for failure to tender periodic dues and initiation fees. To summarize, an employee cannot be compelled under a union-security clause to become a member of the union, nor can he be forced to remain a member in order to hold his job. He can only be compelled to pay his dues and initiation fee.

The Supreme Court has explained this result by referring to the legislative history behind the amendment of Section 8(a)(3) to permit union-security arrangements:

> These additions were intended to accomplish twin purposes. On the one hand, the most serious abuses of compulsory unionism were eliminated by abolishing the closed shop. On the other hand, Congress recognized that in the absence of a union-security provision "many employees sharing the benefits of what unions are able to accomplish, by collective bargaining, will refuse to pay their share of the cost." Consequently, under the new law "employers would still be permitted to enter into agreements requiring all employees in a given bargaining unit to become members thirty days after being hired" but "expulsion from a union cannot be a ground of compulsory discharge if the worker is not delinquent in paying his initiation fees or dues." The amendments were intended only to "remedy the most serious abuses of compulsory union membership and yet give employers and unions who feel that such agreements promoted stability by eliminating 'free riders' the right to continue such arrangements." [5]

But don't many union-security provisions explicitly require an employee to join a union as a condition of employment?

Yes. But these provisions are misleading and cannot be enforced according to their literal meaning. A typical union-security clause looks like this:

It shall be a condition of employment that all employees covered by this agreement shall become and remain members of the union in good standing on or before the thirtieth day after this contract is signed, and all new employees covered by this agreement shall become and remain members of the union in good standing on or before the thirtieth day after their first day of work.

However, as indicated in the answer to the previous question, the union may require no more under such a clause than the payment of regular dues and initiation fees. The phrase "become and remain members of the union" must be read as requiring "membership" only as the courts have defined the term: that is, fulfilling the bare financial obligations of membership.

What's the difference between full membership and statutory membership?

In these questions and answers, we refer to the minimum financial obligations of membership that may be required under a union-security clause as the "statutory" obligations of membership. A person who pays his dues and initiation fees pursuant to a "statutory" union-security clause assumes only the statutory obligations of union membership. An employee who assumes the full obligations of union membership—that is, agrees to join the union—is referred to as a "full" union member.

What are the obligations of an employee who joins a union under the mistaken belief that full union membership is required?

The law in this area is unsettled. An employee could certainly argue that if he joined a union in the mistaken belief that full membership is required by a union-security clause, he should be allowed to drop his full membership and assume only the statutory obligations of membership. But there is no case law specifically permitting this. It is also unsettled whether there is any affirmative duty imposed upon a union, particularly under the duty of fair representation, to accurately advise employees that their only obligation under a union-security clause is to assume statutory membership.[6] However, if an employee asked the union whether he was required to join the union as a condition of employment, and received a misleading answer, he would have a strong claim that he is entitled to drop his full membership.

What if the union denies membership to the employee or suspends or expels the employee from union membership?

The NLRA is quite explicit on this point. As indicated earlier, under a proviso to Section 8(a)(3) the employer may discharge an employee under a union-security clause only if the employee fails to tender the union dues and initiation fees.[7] This rule applies even to an employee who has voluntarily assumed full union membership and not merely the statutory obligation to pay his dues and initiation fees. This means, for example, that an employee who is expelled from the union for espousing the claim of a rival union may not be deprived of his job on this account. Nor may an employer validly discharge an employee under a union-security clause if the employee was fined by the union and refused to pay the fine, or even if the employee was expelled from the union for refusing to pay the fine. Depending upon the union constitution, the union may have the right in such a case to expel the member for failure to pay a fine, or to enforce the collection of the fine through legal proceedings. However, under

Section 8(a)(3) the union cannot require the termination of the member's employment in such a case. Similarly, an employee who refuses to take an oath of membership, who is delinquent in attending union meetings, or who violates some union rule, such as prohibition against crossing a picket line, may be subject to internal union discipline, but not to discharge under a union-security clause.[8] If the union does not expel the member in such cases, it may continue to require him to pay his periodic dues and initiation fees. So long as the employee offers to pay his periodic dues and initiation fee he may not be fired.[9] Even if the union refuses to accept the employee's payment of dues, he is protected under this proviso if he "tenders" them—that is, offers to pay them.

If the employer has "reasonable grounds" for believing that union membership was denied or terminated for reasons other than the failure to pay dues and initiation fees, he may not fire the employee.[10] This provision is designed to protect the employer who is caught in the middle of a claim by the union that the employee was dropped from union membership for failure to pay his dues and a claim by the employee that his union membership was terminated for some other reason. It also protects the employee from sudden discharge where there is a dispute about why he was dropped from the union. On the other hand, if the individual fails to pay his dues and initiation fee, once the union makes a valid demand for his discharge, he cannot save his job by a later payment of the amounts owed. This rule is followed in the belief that otherwise the employer might delay its obligation to discharge the employee in order to give him a chance to satisfy his debt to the union, and this would hamper the union's legitimate interest in prompt enforcement of union-security arrangements.[11]

The union may require discharging the employee only for failure to pay what are properly considered regular and normal dues and initiation fees. This means that the union cannot require the discharge of an employee who refuses to pay higher dues than normally required of all members, dues which include a portion that is rebated if the member attends meetings regularly, an excessive initiation fee, penalties, fines, or special assessments.[12]

How does a statutory union-security clause differ from an "agency-shop" provision?

The "agency shop" is a form of a union-security clause that requires the employee to pay dues and initiation fees as a condition of employment, but does not require membership. Given the Supreme Court's interpretation of an employee's limited membership obligation under a union-security clause, there is little practical difference to the employee between a statutory union-security agreement and an agency-shop provision. Even if the agency-shop and statutory union-security agreement are theoretically the same, the union may prefer to negotiate a clause requiring membership as a condition of employment in order to enhance its prestige and status as bargaining agent. Moreover, the typical union-security provision provides by its plain terms that an employee must join the union to keep his job. The employee is not likely to know that under the law the union cannot compel him to be a member, but can only require him to pay dues and initiation fees as a condition of employment. As already indicated, this may result in an unintentional assumption by the employee of full, rather than statutory, union membership. This is not likely to occur under an agency-shop provision, which makes no mention of union membership.

There is also a third form of union-security provision—the "maintenance-of-membership" clause—which is less common than the two already discussed. It simply provides that any person presently a member of the union must continue to be a member in order to retain his job. It does not require a nonmember to join the union as a condition of employment. Under this type of clause, which merely attempts to continue membership that was at one time voluntary, an employee cannot, of course, be compelled to do more than pay his dues and initiation fees as a condition of employment.

What is the rule as to union-security provisions in the case of public employees?

This varies from state to state and between state and federal employment. Some states permit the negotiation of agency-shop provisions, but most prohibit the typical private-sector union-security arrangement.[13] All forms of union security are prohibited in federal employment.[14]

What are the remedies if the union improperly forces the discharge of an employee under a union-security clause?

The NLRB may order the reinstatement of the employee and require the employer or the union to compensate the employee for lost earnings.[15] But the employee must be very careful not to be tripped up by some important procedural rules. In the first place, the Supreme Court has held that the only place to make a claim of an improper discharge under a union security clause is before the National Labor Relations Board.[16] The NLRB operates under a strict statute of limitations of six months from the time of the action that is claimed to be improper.[17]

The leading case on this subject is quite instructive.[18] An employee failed to pay his dues to his union on time and the union required his discharge under a valid union-security clause. The member claimed, however, that under the union constitution, particularly as interpreted in the past, late payment of a few months did not result in termination of employment. The employee sued the union in state court and won a substantial monetary recovery. But the Supreme Court reversed on the ground that only the NLRB had jurisdiction to decide a claim that involved a union-security clause under 8(a)(3) of the NLRA. By this time it was too late for the employee to bring an action before the NLRB.

May an employee terminate his union membership at any time?

It is not clear. Traditionally, union constitutions had no provisions for resignation. An employee could terminate his membership automatically by refusing to pay dues or refusing to pay a fine. The question whether he could resign had little practical significance. However, in recent years, some unions have sued members to collect fines, particularly fines imposed for crossing picket lines.[19] In such cases the member may attempt to resign from the union before crossing the picket line, in order to escape his obligations under the union constitution.[20] In these cases the courts have held that if the union affords no mechanism for resignation, the employee can terminate his membership at will simply by notifying the union.[21] Some unions have responded to this by adopting constitutional provisions that limit the times and circumstances under which a member may resign, in some cases permitting resignation only during certain limited periods of the membership year or prohibiting resignation during a strike.

Whether a union, by its constitution, can limit the member's right to resign, and what reasonable procedures may be imposed upon the member in order to terminate membership, have not been decided by the courts.[22]

What is the effect of a "right-to-work" law on the union-security arrangements discussed so far?

Congress has permitted states to enact legislation that makes it unlawful for a union and employer to agree to a clause requiring union membership as a condition of employment.[23] A state may also prohibit an agency-shop arrangement.[24] A union may not lawfully make a bargaining demand that the employer grant such a clause in a right-to-work state. The question of right-to-work legislation is a volatile political issue, and Congress has not yielded to pressure from unions and others to drop the right-to-work provision of the NLRA.[25] Only a minority of states have enacted right-to-work legislation.[26]

May the union require the employer to withhold an employee's union dues from her paycheck and turn them over to the union?

Only if the employee consents to this arrangement. The law permits the union and employer to agree to a "checkoff" clause. Under such a provision, when an employee voluntarily consents to such an arrangement, the employer will withhold from her paycheck the amount of her union dues and pay those directly to the union. However, the authorization to deduct dues must be in writing, and the employee must have the option to terminate it at least once a year.[27] The employee who is bound under a union-security agreement to pay union dues may prefer to have them withheld under a checkoff arrangement. This eliminates any danger that the employee may be terminated from employment for failure to pay dues to the union.

May a union negotiate an agreement that the employer hire employees only through a union-operated hiring hall?

Yes. In certain industries, particularly construction and maritime, it may be difficult and impractical for the employer to do the hiring. For example, where the crew of a large ocean-going liner substantially changes with each cruise, it may make more sense for hiring to be done in a centralized place where all active employees in the industry may register for employment and all employers may post job openings. Thus, in both the industries mentioned, as well as others, the employers and union may agree that hiring will be done, often exclusively, through a hiring hall operated by the union. Typically, available jobs are awarded through a bidding procedure, with priority going to employees who have the greatest seniority or who have been out of work the longest.[28]

In upholding the validity of a hiring-hall arrangement under the NLRA, the Supreme Court recognized the possibility that it might result in favoritism towards union members in employment referrals. However, the Court stated:

The hiring hall at times has been a useful adjunct to the closed shop. But Congress may have thought that it need not serve that cause, that in fact it has served well both labor and management —particularly in the maritime field and in the building and construction industry. In the latter the contractor who frequently is a stranger to the area where the work is done requires a "central source" for his employment needs; and a man looking for a job finds in the hiring hall "at least a minimum guarantee of continued employment." . . .

It may be that the very existence of the hiring hall encourages union membership. We may assume that it does. The very existence of the union has the same influence. . . . The truth is that the union is a service agency that probably encourages membership whenever it does its job well.[29]

The Court concluded that if there is no specific proof that the employee was discriminated against in the use of the hiring hall, the hiring hall would not be deemed unlawful. While conceding that hiring halls might "need more regulation than the Act presently affords," the Court concluded that any such regulation would have to come from Congress and not from the courts.

At the time of the above decision the NLRB had uniformly required the parties to a hiring hall arrangement to include in their agreement a provision that expressly forbade the union to discriminate against nonunion members in making referrals. Most hiring hall agreements routinely include such a clause. But it is unclear from the Court's decision whether such a clause is still required.

A hiring hall arrangement may not be limited to union members, for that would violate Section 8(a)(3) by effectively creating a closed shop. The nonunion member must be allowed to use the hiring hall and receive referrals on a nondiscriminatory basis, but the union may charge the nonmember a service fee for the use of the hiring hall.[30]

Hiring-hall arrangements often provide for classifications among employees. For example, in the maritime industry, priority is given in hiring to those who have already shipped over those who have never been employed in the industry. These kinds of classifications have been challenged as favoring the hiring of union members (since, for example, all employees who have shipped will probably be union members under union-security clauses), but, for the most part, these classifications have been upheld by the courts.[31]

May a union and employer give favored treatment under a collective-bargaining agreement to union stewards?

In certain cases, yes. Many collective-bargaining agreements give favored treatment to union stewards—for example, providing that the steward has top seniority in his department. In a recent decision, the NLRB concluded that in general a contract clause that favors union stewards violates the NLRA by in effect encouraging union membership, because, as a practical matter, shop stewards are chosen from among active union members. However, the NLRB recognized that all employees in the bargaining unit benefit if there is infrequent turnover in the job of steward. Thus the NLRB will permit granting of extra seniority to shop stewards if the seniority is limited to layoff and recall. Extra seniority for other purposes, such as vacation benefits or bidding rights to other jobs, cannot lawfully be granted to shop stewards.[32]

NOTES

1. NLRA § 8(a)(3), particularly the clauses that begin "Provided" and "Provided further." In the construction industry a shorter "grace period" is provided; an employee may be required as a condition of employment to join the union within seven days of the beginning of employment. A union may lawfully negotiate such a provision even if it has not yet

established its majority status as bargaining representative, NLRA §8(f). For a more complete discussion of § 8(f), *see* NLRB v. Iron Workers Local 103, 434 U.S. 335 (1978).

2. *Ibid.*

3. NLRA §§ 9(e)(1), (2).

4. NLRB v. General Motors Corp., 373 U.S. 734, 742 (1963). *See also* Radio Officers Union v. NLRB, 347 U.S. 17, 41 (1954), in which the Court states that the "legislative history clearly indicates that Congress intended to prevent utilization of union security agreements for any purpose other than to compel payment of union dues and fees."

This judicial gloss on the statute is helpful in insulating the individual's job rights, for the statute is not quite so clear on this point. Under part (B) of the second proviso to Section 8(a)(3), it is quite plain that if union membership is denied or terminated for reasons other than failure to pay dues and initiation fees, the employee cannot be discharged. But part (A) of the same proviso, by referring to the availability of union membership, implies that the employee must at least apply for union membership and join the union if accepted. However, cases like *Radio Officers* above, and Union Starch & Ref. Co., 87 NLRB 779 (1949), *enf'd*, 186 F.2d 1008 (7th Cir. 1951), *cert. denied*, 342 U.S. 815 (1951), hold that the employee need not apply for union membership or participate in any way in union activities to hold his job under 8(a)(3).

In the *General Motors* decision, the Court said "Of course, if the union chooses to extend membership even though the employee will meet only the minimum financial burden, and refuses to support or 'join' the union in any other affirmative way, the employee may have to become a 'member' under a union shop contract, in the sense that the union may be able to place him on its rolls." 373 U.S. at 743–44.

See also Molders Local 125, 178 NLRB 208 (1969). *See generally* Atleson, *Union Fines and*

Picket Lines, 17 U.C.L.A. L. Rev. 681, 717–20; Toner, *The Union Shop under Taft-Hartley,* 5 Lab. L. J. 552 (1954).

5. NLRB v. General Motors Corp., *supra* note 4, at 734, 740–41. Under Title VII of the Civil Rights Act an employee may be excused from payment of dues and initiation fee on religious grounds, *see* Burns v. So. Pac. Transp. Co., 17 FEP Cases 1648 (9th Cir. 1978), *cert. denied,* 47 LW 3457 (1-9-79). *Compare* Buckley v. AFTRA, 496 F.2d 305 (2nd Cir. 1974), *cert. denied,* 419 U.S. 1093 (1974) in which a claim of immunity from membership on First Amendment grounds is raised unsuccessfully.

6. There are cases that require a union to abide by its duty of fair representation in honoring employees' requests not to have their dues used for political purposes, *e.g.* Ellis v. Ry. Clerks Union, 91 LRRM 2339 (S.D. Cal. 1976); Seay v. McDonnell-Douglas Corp., 553 F.2d 1126 (9th Cir. 1976). It would seem that the rule of these cases should apply by analogy and require a union to advise an employee that he need not assume full membership to hold his job. The question of use of dues for political purposes is discussed more fully in Chapter IX. *But see* Lodge 702, IAM v. Loudermilk, 444 F.2d 719 (5th Cir. 1971), which suggests that it is an open question under the Railway Labor Act whether a union may lawfully fine an employee who joined a union under the mistaken compulsion of a union-security clause.

7. NLRA § 8(a)(3), particularly subclauses (A) and (B) of the clause beginning "Provided further."

8. *E.g.,* Union Starch & Ref. Co., *supra* note 4, (employee cannot be discharged for refusal to file union application forms, attend union meetings, or take union oath); NLRB v. Machinists Union, 203 F.2d 173 (employee cannot be discharged where he is charged with "dual unionism," and expelled from the union and fined on that account, but tenders his monthly dues). *See also* NLRB v. Hershey Foods Corp., 513 F.2d 1083 (9th Cir. 1975) for a listing

of major decisions on these questions. *But see* Local 171, Ass'n of Pulp & Paper Workers, 165 NLRB 971 (1967), permitting a union to require the discharge under Section 8(a)(3) of an employee who refused to pay dues where a portion of the dues was refunded for regular attendance at union meetings. The NLRB reversed an earlier decision in NLRB v. Leece-Neville Co., 140 NLRB 56 (1963), *enf'd*, 330 F.2d 242 (6th Cir. 1964), *cert. denied*, 379 U.S. 819 (1964), that such an arrangement in effect constituted a fine for nonattendance at union meetings. On the question generally of a union's right to impose fines, *see* NLRB v. Allis-Chalmers Mfg. Co., 388 U.S. 175 (1967).

9. Steelworkers Local 4186, 181 NLRB 992 (1970).

10. See the statutory references in note 7, *supra.*

11. General Motors Corp., 134 NLRB 1107 (1961).

12. *See, e.g.* Electric Auto-Lite Co., 92 NLRB 1073 (1950), *enf'd*, NLRB v. Electric Auto-Lite Co., 196 F.2d 500 (6th Cir. 1952), *cert. denied*, 344 U.S. 823 1952) (system of dues rebate for attending union meetings was in effect a fine for nonattendance); Painters Local 1627, 233 NLRB 118 (1977) (failure to pay union fine cannot be lawful basis for refusing to hire an employee). Excessive initiation fees are directly prohibited by the NLRA in § 8(b)(5), making it unlawful for the union to require payment under a union-security agreement of an initiation fee "which the Board finds excessive or discriminatory under all the circumstances." The NLRB looks to practices among unions in the industry to make this determination. *See, e.g.,* Television and Radio Broadcasting Studio Employees, Local 804, 315 F.2d 398 (3rd Cir. 1963). *See also* Burch v. International Ass'n of Machinists, (5th Cir. 1971), in which the union's failure to follow a consistent and rational pattern in handling membership cancellations where dues payments lapsed required reinstatement of the member. *Compare* Auto Workers, Local 1756, 100 LRRM 1208 (1979), in which an initiation or read-

mission fee imposed by a union upon an employee who had resigned his membership was held unlawful.

13. Government Employee Relations Report, 51:501 *et seq.* (1977). *See also* SMITH, EDWARDS AND CLARK, LABOR RELATIONS LAW IN THE PUBLIC SECTOR 595–97 (1974). *See* Abood v. Detroit Bd of Educ., 431 U.S. 209 (1977), upholding the constitutionality of an agency-shop arrangement in the public sector.

14. Exec. Order No. 11,491, § 12(c), 34 Fed. Reg. 17,605 (1969), as amended by Exec. Order No. 11,616, 36 Fed. Reg. 17,319 (1971).

15. NLRA § 10(c).

16. Amalgamated Ass'n of Ry. Employees v. Lockridge, 403 U.S. 274 (1971).

17. NLRA § 10(b).

18. Amalgamated Ass'n v. Lockridge, *supra* note 16.

19. The leading case upholding the union's right under the NLRA to collect a fine is NLRB v. Allis-Chalmers, *supra* note 8. The legality of union fines is discussed in Chapter II.

20. Booster Lodge 405, Machinists v. NLRB, 412 U.S. 84 (1973).

21. NLRB v. Granite State Bd. Textile Workers, 409 U.S. 213 (1972).

22. Booster Lodge 405 Machinists v. NLRB, *supra* note 20.

23. NLRA § 14(b).

24. Retail Clerks Local 1625 v. Schermerhorn 373 U.S. 746 (1963). The Court left open the question whether a right-to-work statute could prohibit a union-security provision less stringent than an agency shop.

25. The last sustained efforts to repeal 14(b) failed. The House of Representatives passed a repealer in 1965, H.R. 77, 89th Cong., 1st Sess. The Labor Reform Act of 1977 did not include repeal of 14(b), although it was sought by unions. *See* P. SULTAN, RIGHT-TO-WORK LAWS: A STUDY IN CONFLICT (1958); Grodin and Beeson, *State Right-to-Work Laws and Federal Labor Policy*, 52 CALIF. L. REV. 95 (1964); Pollett, *Right to Work Law Issues: An*

Evidentiary Approach, 37 N.C.L. REV. 233 (1959).

26. The list presently includes Alabama, Arizona, Arkansas, Florida, Georgia, Iowa, Kansas, Mississippi, Nebraska, Nevada, New Hampshire, North Carolina, North Dakota, South Carolina, South Dakota, Tennessee, Texas, Utah, Virginia, and Wyoming. *See* Oil Workers v. Mobil Oil Corp., 426 U.S. 407 (1976), dealing with the question whether a state has adequate contacts with the employment relationship to impose its right-to-work statute.

27. LMRA § 302(2)(C).

28. *See* NLRA § 8(b)(4) *and* Interstate Electric Co., 227 NLRB 1996 (1977). *In* Teamsters Local 174, 226 NLRB 690 (1976), the board held that a hiring-hall arrangement, to be valid, must have some rational standards for making referrals. For useful descriptions of how hiring halls work see Samoff, *Taft-Hartley Job Discrimination Victories,* 17 LAB. L. J. 643 (1966), an empirical study of litigation involving hiring halls. *See also Hearings on Hiring Halls in the Maritime Industry, Subcomm. on Labor-Management Relations of the Senate Comm. on Labor and Public Welfare,* 81st Cong., 2d Sess. (1950); GOLDBERG, THE MARITIME STORY (1958); Sherman, *The Legal Status of the Building and Construction Trades Unions in the Hiring Process,* 47 GEO. L. J. 203 (1958).

29. Local 357, Teamsters v. NLRB, 365 U.S. 667, 672–673 (1961). The hiring hall is not a union-security device prohibited under § 14(b), Houston Chapter, Assoc. Gen. Contractors, 143 NLRB 409 (1963), enf'd 349 F.2d 449 (5th Cir. 1965).

30. Mountain Pacific Chapter of Associated General Contractors, 119 NLRB 883 (1970). The NLRB required as a condition of upholding a hiring-hall agreement that it explicitly provide for nondiscriminatory referrals and give the employer the right to reject any applicant referred by the union, and that the agreement be posted so that employees could see the safeguards provided.

31. *See, e.g.* Interstate Electric Co., *supra* note 28. *But compare* Teamsters Local 174, *supra* note 28 (union must apply some rational standard of referral; arbitrary referrals will not do); Iron Workers Local 433, 228 NLRB 1231 (1977) (union owes duty of fair representation to employees in making referrals—threat to pound employee's head in the pavement interferes with his protected rights!). See GOLDBERG, *supra* note 28. Compare NLRB v. Electrical Workers, Local 322, No. 92 Daily Labor Report page D-1 (BNA) (10th Cir. 1979).

32. The leading case on this question is Dairylea Cooperative, Inc., 219 NLRB 656 (1975). *See also* Pattern Makers Assoc. of Detroit, 233 NLRB 77 (1977); Perfection Automotive Products, 232 NLRB 109 (1977).

IX

Political Activities of Unions and Union Members

One of the most important rights of union members is the preservation of individual political freedom. The questions and answers in this chapter deal with three ways in which the law protects the political rights of union members. First, a union member cannot be disciplined or penalized for engaging in political activity, whether within or outside the union. Second, an employee cannot be compelled to support, financially or otherwise, political causes or activities of the union which he opposes. Finally, the law minimizes the overall impact of the union upon the political process by restricting the union's spending of money for certain political activities.

How does the law protect the individual's right to engage in political activity?

The LMRDA guarantees a broad right to engage in political activity without restraint by the union. Section 101(a)(2) of the LMRDA secures certain basic political rights of members of labor organizations. These

157

include freedom of assembly and expression, both as to internal union affairs and matters of general concern. These protections are subject only to the union's right to make reasonable rules to enforce the responsibility of the member to his union and to restrain the member from interfering with the union's performance of its legal and contractual obligations.[1]

The extent of this protection is illustrated by a case in which members of the union campaigned for the enactment in their state of a right-to-work law.[2] The union expelled them for violating a provision of the union constitution that condemned "conduct unbecoming a member." The court recognized a number of situations in which a member's conduct would not be protected because it jeopardized the union's existence as an institution—for example, engaging in spying on the union on behalf of an employer, dual unionism, violation of work rules, and wildcat strikes. While the campaign to enact a right-to-work law might not have been in the union's best interests as an institution, the court nevertheless held that the union could not expel the members on this basis:

This brings us to the question of the nature of the political doctrine propounded and the manner in which it is advocated. We are not called upon to decide what the result would be if a member was expelled for advocating repeal of the Wagner Act or the abolition of unions. Only the right-to-work law is here involved. The union argues that it may reasonably consider such a law seriously inimical to its interests. This is certainly not an unreasonable position, and, in addition to the DeMille case, many authorities agree. But there is substantial respectable opinion to the contrary. [Professor] Cox says, "The member who acts as a strikebreaker may be guilty of treason, but one can believe in right-to-work laws and remain a good trade-unionist." . . . There being such a disparity of opinion as to the long-run effect of voluntary unionism, the question becomes not whether the union is justified in its opinion, but whether the point is sufficiently debatable so that society's interest in the debate, together with the individual's right to speak freely on political matters, outweighs the union's interest in subduing public dissent among union members.[3]

In another well-known case, involving remarks by a union member that allegedly defamed an officer of the union, the court put the proposition in a slightly different way:

In a proviso to Section 101(a)(2), there are two exceptions to the broad rule of free expression. . . . We believe that Congress intended only those exceptions which were expressed. . . .
So far as union discipline is concerned, Salzhandler had a right to speak his mind and spread his opinions regarding the union's officers, regardless of whether his statements were true or false.[4]

While the union official who thinks he is defamed may sue in court for defamation of character, he may not use the powers of the union against the individual who speaks out against him.[5]

Do the rights of political freedom extend to officers as well as members of the union?

With one exception, the answer is yes. The cases make clear that an officer of a union is entitled to the same protection as any other member against discipline for engaging in political activities. For example, in the course of the election campaign in the Mine Workers Union, Yablonski, the insurgent candidate, was removed by Boyle from his appointed position as acting director of a political arm of the union. The court held that his removal from office was a reprisal for his candidacy, and was prohibited under the LMRDA. The court held that the act "guarantees union members a full right to participate in the political affairs of their union and requires elected union officials to act without abusing their positions of trust." [6] If the officer is removed for reasons unrelated to his political activity, he has no right under the act, but courts are quick to find that the real motive for removal was the member's political activity.

The principal exception to the rule that union officials cannot be disciplined for political activities is in the case of a rule adopted by the union and uniformly applied to prohibit all political activity by union officials. The law recognizes that a union may properly conclude that its intersts are best served if it insists on political neutrality on the part of all its elected and appointed officials.[7] But if such a rule is really used to curb particular political activity that the union leadership does not like, then the discipline or removal of the officer violates the act.

May a union spend a member's dues for political purposes?

In certain situations, a member may prevent her union from spending her dues for political activities. Congress has made the judgment, discussed in greater detail in Chapter VIII, that a union may not compel an employee to become a member of the union in order to keep her job. But because all employees in the bargaining unit benefit from the union's representation,

Congress has permitted unions to require an employee to pay the equivalent of dues and initiation fees to the union as a condition of keeping her job. This "financial core" of compulsory union membership is in effect a "service fee," designed to cover the union's costs in representing the individual. Under this theory, an employee who is required to pay dues and an initiation fee to a union has the right to insist that these monies be used only for purposes of representation within the bargaining unit.

In dealing with this problem, the Supreme Court said in a case that arose under the Railway Labor Act:

> Congress did not completely abandon the policy of full freedom of choice embodied in the 1934 Act [the Railway Labor Act], but rather made inroads on it for the limited purpose of eliminating the problems created by the "free rider." . . . We respect this congressional purpose when we construe [the statute] as not vesting the unions with unlimited power to spend exacted money. We are not called upon to delineate the precise limits of that power in this case. We have before us only the question whether the power is restricted to the extent of denying the unions the right, over the employee's objection, to use his money to support political causes which he opposes. Its use to support candidates for public office, and advance political programs, is not a use which helps defray the expenses of the negotiation or administration of collective agreements, or the expenses entailed in the adjustment of grievances and disputes.[8]

The key cases on this question all involved individuals who claimed that they were members of the union only because they were required to join under a union-security clause. It is not clear from the cases whether a person who voluntarily joins the union may similarly object to the expenditure of her dues for political purposes. It may be argued that under the contractual theory of union membership, the voluntary full member agrees to support whatever activities the majority decides to undertake.[9]

What constitutes an expenditure for political purposes?

This question is quite unsettled. Surely expenditures to support candidates for public office and political parties are the kinds of political expenditures that an individual member may not be compelled to make. The courts have also indicated that "political causes" and "political programs" are to be treated the same way, but the reported cases have not defined precisely what those terms mean. Some justices of the Supreme Court have argued, in dissent, that many so-called "political" programs—such as lobbying for changes in the minimum-wage law, or for protective tariffs—relate directly to the everyday collective-bargaining responsibilities of the union, and are normal and accepted functions of unions.[10]

The problem is complicated by the fact that while the major cases address only the problem of political expenditures, the theory behind the cases is that the individual who is forced to join a union under a statutory union-security clause should be required to pay dues only for the basic costs of representation in collective bargaining. Thus it remains to be seen whether a member may prevent a union from spending his dues for purposes which, while not political in nature, go beyond the normal expenditures of collective bargaining.[11]

Because of the uncertainty as to the *types* of union

spending to which a union member may object, the cases have turned upon the *procedures* a member must follow in objecting to union expenditures.

What procedures must a member follow in order to restrict union expenditures of her dues?

The courts have held that an individual may not complain of the expenditure of union dues for political purposes unless she first makes clear that she objects to such spending. The member need only make a general objection to use of her funds for political expenditures, and need not specify exactly what political activities she opposes.[12]

If the union continues to make expenditures for political purposes over the member's objection, she may compel the union to refund the portion of her dues that was used for political purposes. Further, once it is determined what portion of her dues is being used for political purpose, the objecting member may have her future dues reduced proportionately. In either case, the union has the burden of calculating the portion of union dues that is used for other than political purposes; the individual does not have the burden of establishing the extent of expenditures for political purposes.[13]

Because these calculations are so difficult to make, and the definition of "political activities" so uncertain, unions have been encouraged to devise their own rules and procedures for permitting a member to object to union spending of her dues. Where a union establishes reasonable procedures with appropriate safeguards for the individual, the member must comply with these procedures before being given relief in court.[14] Some courts have imposed a duty of fair representation upon unions in advising employees how they may utilize these procedures.[15]

The individual's only remedy is to obtain some proportionate relief in the manner described above. The member may not refuse to pay her dues altogether on the ground that a portion of the dues is being used for political purposes, nor may she prevent the union from making these expenditures.

Does the law restrict the use of membership dues for political purposes even where the member consents?

Yes. The Federal Election Campaign Act limits the right of a labor organization to make political contributions or expenditures for any election to federal office.[16] These provisions generally place unions under the same kinds of limitation as corporations with regard to political spending. The union may not use its general funds to make contributions in connection with a federal election or to make expenditures directed at the general public. For example, the union may not purchase television time to conduct a get-out-the-vote campaign directed to the public at large. On the other hand, the union may spend money to communicate with its own members on any subject, including electioneering on behalf of candidates for public office. It may conduct registration and get-out-the-vote drives aimed at its members and their families. The union may also use its funds for general educational campaigns directed at the public—for example, a campaign urging repeal of the right-to-work provision of the Taft-Hartley law.

State laws may also have a bearing upon union expenditures. Thus, a state law may limit union contributions and expenditures for state and local elections in the same way that the federal law regulates spending for federal elections. If there is no such law, the union is free to make expenditures and contributions for state and local candidates.

But even if the state or federal law permits the union to make election expenditures, the individual union member still has the right to object to the expenditure of his dues for political purposes, as discussed earlier.

May the union engage in political activities through voluntary fund-raising?

Yes. The Supreme Court has held,[17] and the Federal Election Campaign Act provides,[18] that a union may set up an independent fund, wholly separate from the union's regular treasury, for the purpose of supporting political candidates and issues. However, contributions to these funds must be wholly voluntary and cannot be a condition of employment or of union membership. In a recent case a union required employees who joined the union to agree to a deduction of $1.00 per year for political contributions. The member could have the contribution refunded if he filed a separate written request. Such a "reverse check-off" system was held unlawful under the Federal Election Campaign Act.[19]

While the political fund must be a fiscally separate entity, it may be administered by officials of the union, and general union funds may be used to establish and maintain the fund. Under the Federal Election Campaign Act, there are some limitations on the expenditures that may be made through these funds—for example, there is a dollar ceiling on contributions that may be made on behalf of each candidate.[20]

NOTES

1. LMRDA § 101(a)(1).
2. Mitchell v. International Ass'n of Machinists, 16 Cal. Rptr. 813 (1961).
3. *Ibid.* 16 Cal. Rptr. at 819.

4. Salzhandler v. Caputo, 316 F.2d 445, 450, 451 (2nd Cir. 1963), *cert. denied,* 375 U.S. 946 (1963).
5. *Ibid.* The case is discussed in Chapter III.
6. Yablonski v. Mine Workers Union, 71 LRRM 3041 (D.D.C. 1969).
7. See Navarro v. Leu, 101 LRRM 2057 (N.D. Ohio, 1979).
8. International Ass'n of Machinists v. Street, 367 U.S. 740 (1961).
9. Justice Black dissenting, *ibid.* at 780, 788–89.
10. *See* the dissenting opinion of Justice Frankfurter in the *Street* case, *ibid.* at 797, 812–16.
11. *See* Summers, *Labor Law Decisions of the 1962 Supreme Court Term,* 1963–1964 PROCEEDINGS OF A.B.A. SECTION ON LABOR RELATIONS LAW 1, 12–14. *Compare* Gabauer v. Woodcock, 100 LRRM 2366 (8th Cir. 1979).
12. Railway Clerks Union v. Allen, 373 U.S. 113, 118–19 (1963). *See also* International Ass'n of Machinists v. Street, *supra* note 9; *compare* Seay v. McDonnell-Douglas Corp., 533 F.2d 1126 (9th Cir. 1976).
13. Railway Clerks v. Allen, *supra* note 13, at 121–22.
14. *Ibid.* at 122–24.
15. Ellis v. Railway Clerks Union, 91 LRRM 2339 (S.D. Calif. 1976); Seay v. McDonnell-Douglas, *supra* note 13.
16. Federal Election Campaign Act Amendments of 1976, Pub. L. No. 94-283, § 101, 90 Stat. 475, 486–92, 2 U.S.C.A. §§ 431 et seq. *See* Comment, *The Regulation of Union Political Activity: Majority and Minority Rights and Remedies,* 126 U. PA. L. REV. 386 (1977).
17. *See* Pipefitters Local 562 v. United States, 407 U.S. 385 (1972).
18. Federal Election Campaign Act, *supra* note 17, especially 2 U.S.C.A. §§ 432, 433, 434.
19. Federal Election Comm. v. National Education Ass'n, 99 LRRM 2263, 99 LRRM 3463 (D.D.C. 1978).
20. See Walther v. Federal Election Commission, 101 LRRM 2360 (D.D.C. 1979).

X

The Right to Sue the Union

In the preceding chapters we have examined the various substantive rights enjoyed by union members. In order to vindicate these rights, it may be necessary for the member to bring a legal action against his union, by filing a charge with the National Labor Relations Board or a complaint with the Secretary of Labor, or by instituting a lawsuit in state or federal court. In this chapter we explore whether a union may limit the member's right to sue the union, as well as some practical considerations involving the costs of litigation. Some of these issues—for example, the question whether a member must first exhaust his internal union remedies before suing the union—have been discussed in other chapters.

May a union discipline a member or otherwise prevent him from suing his union?

No. The LMRDA is explicit on this point. Section 101(a)(4), entitled "Protection of the Right to Sue," states that "no labor organization shall limit the right of any member thereof to institute an action in any court, or in a proceeding before any administrative agency. . . ." A union that seeks to thwart the right to sue will generally try to do so in one of two ways: by fining the offending member or by expelling him from the union. Neither approach is permissible under Section 101(a)(4).

One important exception to this rule concerns the discipline of a union member who brings a decertification proceeding before the NLRB to determine whether the majority of the employees in the union wish to continue to be represented by their union. The courts have held that while a member may be *expelled* for filing a decertification petition, on the ground that such an action "attacks the very existence of the union as the exclusive bargaining agent." [1] the union may not *fine* a member for filing a decertification petition.[2] The courts have concluded that the right to fine in such a situation is too coercive, and might thwart the legitimate right of employees to attempt to change their bargaining representative. It is clear, however, that a member may not be disciplined, by fine or expulsion, for bringing a charge of unfair labor practice against the union.[3]

May a union limit the right to sue by requiring the member to first exhaust his internal union remedies?

Yes. Throughout this book we have seen that the member may be required to exhaust reasonable internal union procedures before resorting to legal action. The LMRDA expressly provides that a member "may be required to exhaust reasonable hearing procedures (but not to exceed a four-month lapse of time) within such organization." In the case of challenges under Title IV, the voting-rights section of the LMRDA, the maximum exhaustion period is three months.[4] Once the applicable period has run, the member is free to bring his legal action, even if the internal union procedures have not been completed.

The exhaustion doctrine is designed to give the union an opportunity to straighten out its own internal problems before courts or administrative agencies become involved, and thus to "stimulate labor organizations to take the initiative and independently to establish honest and democratic procedures." [5] Use of internal union procedures may limit the flow of litigation in administrative agencies and the courts, and the internal decisions of the union may be of assistance to the court or administrative agency if the matter is litigated. It is clear, however, that the union has no absolute right to insist that the member exhaust his internal appeals procedure. Rather, the exhaustion doctrine is to be applied at the court's discretion. The Supreme Court has held that the phrase that a member "may be required" to exhaust internal union procedures "is not a grant of authority to unions more firmly to police their members, but a statement of policy that the public tribunals whose aid is invoked may in their discretion stay their hands for four months, while the aggrieved person seeks relief within the union." [6] Thus, the court may refuse to get involved in the case if the member has not exhausted his internal remedies, but the court is not required to stay its hand.

In general, courts will not require the member to exhaust his internal union remedies if an internal appeal would be futile, if the union clearly had no right to take the action which the member is challenging in his lawsuit, if the right to appeal is not known to the member, or if valuable rights may be lost while the appeals procedure takes place—for example, where the member seeks judicial relief because the union has limited his right of free speech.[7] In one well-known case the court refused to require a trumpet player, who was expelled from the musicians' union, to exhaust his internal union remedies.[8] The court found that the union viewed him as an "exceptional" threat to the union, that one member of the union's executive board had an "intense personal dislike" for him, that the union had treated him severely in the past when he was brought up on charges, that the union had a strong interest in deciding the case against him, and that the union had already taken a firm position on the issue involved. The court concluded that any internal appeal would be futile. Courts have been reluctant to require exhaustion in cases alleging a breach of the duty of fair representation, particularly if the union constitution does not clearly spell out that internal procedures must first be utilized in such a case.[9]

While a court or administrative agency may refuse to hear a case because the member has not exhausted his internal remedies, the union cannot discipline the member for bringing suit without first exhausting his remedies. For example, an employee filed a charge before the NLRB claiming that the employer violated the NLRA by discharging him at the insistence of the union. The union then brought the complaining member up on charges, asserting that he had violated the union constitution by going to the NLRB before exhausting his union remedies. The employee was found guilty and expelled. The Supreme Court overturned the expulsion, holding that "there should be as great a freedom to ask the Board for relief as there is to petition any other department of government for a redress of grievances." [10] The Court concluded that "there cannot be any justification to make the public processes wait until the union member exhausts internal procedures plainly inadequate to deal with all phases of the complex problems concerning the employer, union and employee member." [11]

In another case a union member who brought a court action to enjoin an arbitration was expelled from his union for failure to exhaust internal remedies. The court invalidated his expulsion, holding that a member would be inhibited in his "right of free access" to the court if he had to fear union discipline in case the court concluded that he should have exhausted his remedies within the union.[12]

Can a union member recover attorney's fees in a lawsuit against the union?

Yes. First, the LMRDA specifically gives courts discretion in certain kinds of cases to award counsel fees and costs of the action to the successful plaintiffs. This discretion is granted in cases in which a member sues to compel the union to comply with its reporting obligations under Title II of the LMRDA [13] or in cases in which a member seeks to enforce the fiduciary responsibilities of union officers under Title V.[14]

In addition to these two specific situations covered by the LMRDA, the courts have followed a developing trend in other fields of law of allowing the recovery of counsel fees in appropriate cases even where there is no statutory authority to do so. In a leading case, a union member was expelled by his union for introducing resolutions critical of the union leadership.[15] He sued the union under Section 102 of the LMRDA, contending that his expulsion violated his free-speech rights. The lower court held in favor of the member, and awarded him counsel fees of $5,500. The Supreme Court upheld the award of counsel fees as within the court's discretion, even though the LMRDA did not specifically permit such recovery in a case alleging a Title I violation. The Court applied a "common benefit" theory, developed in other areas of the law in which counsel fees had been awarded, that where a lawsuit benefits all members of the union, all should bear its costs, rather than having them fall upon one person. The Court said: "When a member is disciplined for the exercise of any of the rights protected by Title I, the rights of all members of the union are threatened. And, by vindicating his own rights, the successful litigant dispels the 'chill' cast upon the rights of others." [16] The Court indicated that counsel fees could also be awarded, in an appropriate case, even where a common benefit is not conferred upon the entire union, but where the union's action against the plaintiff was taken in bad faith.[17] Thus, when a union induced an employer to discharge an employee in violation of a collective-bargaining agreement prohibiting discrimination against nonmembers of the union, the union was held liable for counsel fees in the individual's lawsuit for reinstatement, on the basis of its bad faith.[18]

Counsel fees have also been awarded in election cases. Unions have argued in such cases that the plaintiff who is a candidate for office should not recover counsel fees, as the suit would benefit the individual candidate. The courts have permitted the candidate to recover counsel fees, recognizing that while he may be motivated by self-gain, he also confers a benefit on the union by safeguarding fair elections.[19]

May a union member recover punitive damages from his union?

Yes, except in cases involving claims of breach of the duty of fair representation. As in many areas of the law, the union member may be able to recover punitive damages in addition to his out-of-pocket losses if he can show that the union willfully and intentionally deprived him of his rights. For example, in the election between Yablonski and Boyle for the presidency of the Mine Workers Union (summarized in Appendix B), Boyle dismissed Yablonski from his position as director of the union's legislative office as a reprisal for Yablonski's entrance into the election race. The court concluded that "such action of the defendant Boyle was taken spitefully and with malice" and ordered that punitive damages be awarded in the amount of $3,000.[20]

However, in a recent Supreme Court case, a union breached its duty of fair representation when it ignored an individual's grievance. The Court held that a grievant was not entitled to punitive damages in a duty of fair representation case. It concluded that "the prospect of punitive damages in cases such as this could curtail the broad discretion that Vaca afforded unions in handling grievances." Four concurring justices expressed concern that the majority decision might signal a curtailment of punitive damages in other Landrum-Griffin cases, although the majority disclaimed passing upon this point.[21]

May a union member receive financial assistance from an employer in a suit against his union?

The LMRDA specifically provides in the section entitled "Protection of the Right to Sue" that "no interested employer or employer association shall directly or indirectly finance, encourage, or participate in, except as a party, any such action, proceeding, appearance, or petition." [22]

In a recent case the court held that this section is not applicable to an independent legal aid organization which represents employees in legal actions involving union security issues, even though the organization is financed in part by contributions from employers. As long as the legal aid organization is not controlled by the employers, and can exercise independent judgment, its operation does not violate the LMRDA.[23]

Apart from this case there has been little case law on this question. Difficult questions remain—for example, whether a foundation actually receives significant support from employers, whether those employers are "interested" in the litigation as provided in the act, and whether the Act applies to a case in which the member is defending a lawsuit, rather than initiating it, as in the case where a union sues a member to collect a fine.

Are there any limitations upon the union's right to defend a lawsuit?

Yes. The courts have held that in cases in which a union officer is charged with a breach of his fiduciary duties under LMRDA Title V, he may not use union funds or union counsel to defend himself. As one court put it: "To allow a union officer to use the power and wealth of the very union which he is accused of pilfering, to defend himself against such charges, is totally inconsistent with Congress's effort to eliminate the undesirable element which has been uncovered in the labor-management field." [24]

It is not clear whether this doctrine extends to cases that do not involve violations of a union officer's fiduciary obligations under Title V. If the theory of the courts is to prevent a union officer from using union funds to defend himself against a charge of wrongdoing against his own union, then the rationale should extend to other cases, such as voting, free speech, and fair representation as well.[25]

A second limitation upon the union's right to defend itself is found in cases in which a court has disqualified the union's counsel from representing it in litigation.

Thus, in a suit by Yablonski against the Mine Workers Union for an accounting and restoration of funds under Title V of the LMRDA, the court held that the union could not be represented by its regular counsel, where that counsel had represented Boyle, the president of the union, in numerous other lawsuits—for example, those challenging the validity of his election victory. The court said that even if there were no obvious conflict of interest in union counsel representing the union in this suit and Boyle in others, the union is entitled to "the most objective counsel obtainable." The court concluded that counsel might not be able to objectively assess the union's position in the Title V lawsuit in view of its representation of Boyle in the other matters.[26]

How can a member find competent counsel to represent him in a suit against his union?

In larger cities, competent lawyers have had experience with cases involving the rights of individuals within their union. It may be possible to locate such lawyers by use of the local bar-association referral system or by consulting the reported individual rights cases, which usually list the lawyers for the respective parties, including the lawyer for the individual employee. In some cities, organizations established for the protection of individual-employee rights—for example, the League for Union Democracy, located in New York City—may be helpful. The increased use of advertising by lawyers may enable the individual to locate a lawyer with expertise in this field.

In smaller communities, the problem is more difficult. Generally, those lawyers with expertise in the field of labor relations regularly represent either management or union clients. They are often reluctant to take on cases involving individual-employee rights, for fear of antagonizing their regular clients.

NOTES

1. NLRB v. International Molders Union, 442 F.2d 92, 94 (7th Cir. 1971).
2. Tawas Tube Products, Inc., 151 NLRB 46 (1965).
3. Local 138, Operating Engineers Union and Charles S. Skura, 148 NLRB 679 (1964).
4. LMRDA §§ 101(a)(4), 402(a).
5. Detroy v. American Guild of Variety Artists, 286 F.2d 75, 79 (2nd Cir. 1961).
6. NLRB v. Marine and Shipbuilding Workers Union, 391 U.S. 418, 426 (1964).
7. *See generally* Keeffe Bros. v. Teamsters Local 592, 562 F.2d 298, 302–3 (4th Cir. 1977).
8. Farowitz v. Musicians Union, 241 F. Supp. 895 (S.D. N.Y. 1965).
9. Orphan v. Furnco Construction Corp., 466 F.2d 795 (7th Cir. 1972).
10. NLRB v. Marine and Shipbuilding Workers Union, *supra* note 6, at 424.
11. *Ibid.* at 425.
12. Ryan v. Brotherhood of Electrical Workers, 361 F.2d 942 (7th Cir. 1966).
13. LMRDA § 201(c).
14. LMRDA § 501(b).
15. Hall v. Cole, 412 U.S. 1 (1972).
16. *Ibid.* at 8.
17. *Ibid.* at 15. *See also* Keeffe Bros. v. Teamsters, *supra* note 7 at 306–7.
18. Richardson v. Communication Workers, 530 F.2d 126 (8th Cir. 1976); *see also* Harrison v. United Transportation Union, 530 F.2d 558 (4th Cir. 1975).
19. Yablonski v. Mine Workers Union, 466 F.2d 424 (D.C. Cir. 1972).

20. Yablonski v. Mine Workers Union, 80 LRRM 3435, 81 LRRM 2593 (D.D.C. 1972).
21. Electrical Workers v. Foust, —— U.S. ——, 101 LRRM 2365 (Sup. Ct. 1979); see especially footnote 9.
22. LMRDA § 101(a)(4).
23. Auto Workers Union v. National Right to Work Legal Defense and Education Foundation, 99 LRRM 3181 (D.C. Cir. 1978).
24. Highway Truck Drivers Local v. Cohen, 182 F. Supp. 608 (E.D. Pa. 1960).
25. *See generally* Note, *Counsel Fees for Union Officers under the Fiduciary Provisions of Landrum-Griffin,* 73 YALE L. J. 443 (1964).
26. Yablonski v. Mine Workers Union, 448 F.2d 1175 (D.C. Cir. 1971).

APPENDIX A

Selected Statutory References

LABOR-MANAGEMENT RELATIONS ACT
(National Labor Relations Act [NLRA] as amended by Taft-Hartley and Landrum-Griffin Acts).

Section 7 [Rights of employees to self-organization and concerted activities, and to refrain from such activities] *

Employees shall have the right to self-organization, to form, join, or assist labor organizations, to bargain collectively through representatives of their own choosing, and to engage in other concerted activities for the purpose of collective bargaining or other mutual aid or protection, and shall also have the right to refrain from any or all of such activities except to the extent that such right may be affected by an agreement re-

---

* These bracketed headings have been prepared by the editors to help you see the subject matter of the section selected.

quiring membership in a labor organization as a condition of employment as authorized in section 8(a)(3) of this title.

Section 8(a)(3) [Unfair labor practice for employer to discriminate against employee on account of his union membership; provisions for conditioning employment upon union membership]

(a) It shall be an unfair labor practice for an employer—

(3) by discrimination in regard to hire or tenure of employment or any term or condition of employment to encourage or discourage membership in any labor organization: *Provided,* That nothing in this subchapter, or in any other statute of the United States, shall preclude an employer from making an agreement with a labor organization (not established, maintained, or assisted by any action defined in this subsection as an unfair labor practice) to require as a condition of employment membership therein on or after the thirtieth day following the beginning of such employment or the effective date of such agreement, whichever is the later . . . : *Provided further,* That no employer shall justify any discrimination against an employee for nonmembership in a labor organization (A) if he has reasonable grounds for believing that such membership was not available to the employee on the same terms and conditions generally applicable to other members, or (B) if he has reasonable grounds for believing that membership was denied or terminated for reasons other than the failure of the employee to tender the periodic dues and the initiation fees uniformly required as a condition of acquiring or retaining membership. . . .

Section 8(b)(1) and (2). [Unfair labor practice for union to interfere with employees' rights under Section 7; proviso regarding right of union to prescribe certain internal rules; prohibition against union causing employer to discriminate against employee on account of union membership.]

(b)   It shall be an unfair labor practice for a labor organization or its agents—

(1)   to restrain or coerce (A) employees in the exercise of the rights guaranteed in section 7 of this title: *Provided,* That this paragraph shall not impair the right of a labor organization to prescribe its own rules with respect to the acquisition or retention of membership therein; or (B) an employer in the selection of his representatives for the purposes of collective bargaining or the adjustment of grievances;

(2)   to cause or attempt to cause an employer to discriminate against an employee in violation of subsection (a)(3) of this section or to discriminate against an employee with respect to whom membership in such organization has been denied or terminated on some ground other than his failure to tender the periodic dues and the initiation fees uniformly required as a condition of acquiring or retaining membership. . . .

Section 9(a) [Exclusive status of bargaining representative; right of individual employee to take up own grievance with employer.]

(a) Representatives designated or selected for the purposes of collective bargaining by the majority of the employees in a unit appropriate for such purposes, shall be the exclusive representatives of all the employees in such unit for the purposes of collective bargaining in respect to rates of pay, wages, hours of employment, or other conditions of employment: *Pro-*

vided, That any individual employee or a group of employees shall have the right at any time to present grievances to their employer and to have such grievances adjusted, without the intervention of the bargaining representative, as long as the adjustment is not inconsistent with the terms of a collective-bargaining contract or agreement then in effect: *Provided further,* That the bargaining representative has been given opportunity to be present at such adjustment.

Section 10(b) [Filing of unfair labor practice charge; time limits.]

(b) Whenever it is charged that any person has engaged in or is engaging in any such unfair labor practice, the Board, or any agent or agency designated by the Board for such purposes, shall have power to issue and cause to be served upon such person a complaint stating the charges in that respect, and containing a notice of hearing before the Board or a member thereof, or before a designated agent or agency, at a place therein fixed, not less than five days after the serving of said complaint: *Provided,* That no complaint shall issue based upon any unfair labor practice occurring more than six months prior to the filing of the charge with the Board and the service of a copy thereof upon the person against whom such charge is made, unless the person aggrieved thereby was prevented from filing such charge by reason of service in the armed forces, in which event the six-month period shall be computed from the day of his discharge. . . .

LABOR-MANAGEMENT REPORTING
and
DISCLOSURE ACT of 1959
(LMRDA; Landrum-Griffin).

Editors' note: Because of the central importance of this statute to the body of this book, we have deleted only those sections that are not of general interest or assistance in following the text. We have indicated by a series of four dots (. . . .) where we have eliminated portions of a section or subsection. However, where entire sections and subsections have been deleted, there is no editorial indication of the omission, as this will usually be obvious from the numbering of the sections.

Title I—Bill of Rights of members of labor organizations

101

(a)(1) **Equal rights.**—Every member of a labor organization shall have equal rights and privileges within such organization to nominate candidates, to vote in elections or referendums of the labor organization, to attend membership meetings, and to participate in the deliberations and voting upon the business of such meetings, subject to reasonable rules and regulations in such organization's constitution and bylaws.

(2) **Freedom of speech and assembly.**—Every member of any labor organization shall have the right to meet and assemble freely with other members; and to express any views, arguments, or opinions; and to express at meetings of the labor organization his views, upon candidates in an election of the labor organization or upon any business properly before the meeting, subject to the organization's established and reasonable

rules pertaining to the conduct of meetings: *Provided,* That nothing herein shall be construed to impair the right of a labor organization to adopt and enforce reasonable rules as to the responsibility of every member toward the organization as an institution and to his refraining from conduct that would interfere with its performance of its legal or contractual obligations.

(3). Dues, initiation fees, and assessments.—Except in the case of a federation of national or international labor organizations, the rates of dues and initiation fees payable by members of any labor organization in effect on September 14, 1959 shall not be increased, and no general or special assessment shall be levied upon such members, except—

(A) in the case of a local labor organization, (i) by majority vote by secret ballot of the members in good standing voting at a general or special membership meeting, after reasonable notice of the intention to vote upon such question, or (ii) by majority vote of the members in good standing voting in a membership referendum conducted by secret ballot; or

(B) in the case of a labor organization, other than a local labor organization or a federation of national or international labor organizations, (i) by majority vote of the delegates voting at a regular convention, or at a special convention of such labor organization held upon not less than thirty days' written notice to the principal office of each local or constituent labor organization entitled to such notice, or (ii) by majority vote of the members in good standing of such labor organization voting in a membership referendum conducted by secret ballot, or (iii) by majority vote of the members of the executive board or similar governing body of such labor organization, pursuant to express authority contained in the constitution and bylaws of such labor organization: *Provided,* That such action on the part of the executive board or similar governing body shall be effective only until the next regular convention of such labor organization.

(4) Protection of the right to sue.—No labor organization shall limit the right of any member thereof to institute an action in any court, or in a proceeding before any administrative agency, irrespective of whether or not the labor organization or its officers are named as defendants or respondents in such action or proceeding, or the right of any member of a labor organization to appear as a witness in any judicial, administrative, or legislative proceeding, or to petition any legislature or to communicate with any legislator: *Provided,* That any such member may be required to exhaust reasonable hearing procedures (but not to exceed a four-month lapse of time) within such organization, before instituting legal or administrative proceedings against such organizations or any officer thereof: *And provided further,* That no interested employer or employer association shall directly or indirectly finance, encourage, or participate in, except as a party, any such action, proceeding, appearance, or petition.

(5) Safeguards against improper disciplinary action. —No member of any labor organization may be fined, suspended, expelled, or otherwise disciplined except for nonpayment of dues by such organization or by any officer thereof unless such member has been (A) served with written specific charges; (B) given a reasonable time to prepare his defense; (C) afforded a full and fair hearing.

(b) Any provision of the constitution and bylaws of any labor organization which is inconsistent with the provisions of this section shall be of no force or effect.

102

Any person whose rights secured by the provisions of this subchapter have been infringed by any violation of this subchapter may bring a civil action in a district court of the United States for such relief (including injunctions) as may be appropriate. Any such action against a labor organization shall be brought in the district court of the United States for the district where the alleged violation occurred, or where the principal office of such labor organization is located.

104

It shall be the duty of the secretary or corresponding principal officer of each labor organization, in the case of a local labor organization, to forward a copy of each collective bargaining agreement made by such labor organization with any employer to any employee who requests such a copy and whose rights as such employee are directly affected by such agreement, and in the case of a labor organization other than a local labor organization, to forward a copy of any such agreement to each constituent unit which has members directly affected by such agreement; and such officer shall maintain at the principal office of the labor organization of which he is an officer copies of any such agreement made or received by such labor organization, which copies shall be available for inspection by any member or by any employee whose rights are affected by such agreement. The provisions of section 210 of this title shall be applicable in the enforcement of this section.

105

Every labor organization shall inform its members concerning the provisions of this chapter.

Title II—Reporting by labor organizations, officers and employees of labor organizations, and employers

201. *Report of labor organizations*

(a) Every labor organization shall adopt a constitution and bylaws and shall file a copy thereof with the Secretary, together with a report, signed by its president and secretary or corresponding principal officers, containing the following information—

(1) the name of the labor organization, its mailing address, and any other address at which it maintains its principal office or at which it keeps the records referred to in this subchapter;

(2) the name and title of each of its officers;

(3) the initiation fee or fees required from a new or transferred member and fees for work permits required by the reporting labor organization;

(4) the regular dues or fees or other periodic payments required to remain a member of the reporting labor organization; and

(5) detailed statements, or references to specific provisions of documents filed under this subsection which contain such statements, showing the provision made and procedures followed with respect to each of the following: (A) qualifications for or restrictions on membership, (B) levying of assessments, (C) participation in insurance or other benefit plans, (D) authorization for disbursement of funds of the labor organization, (E) audit of financial transactions of the labor organization, (F) the calling of regular and special meetings, (G) the selection of officers and stewards and of any representatives to other bodies composed of labor organizations' representatives, with a specific statement of the manner in which each officer was elected, appointed, or otherwise selected, (H) discipline or removal of

officers or agents for breaches of their trust, (I) imposition of fines, suspensions, and expulsions of members, including the grounds for such action and any provision made for notice, hearing, judgment on the evidence, and appeal procedures, (J) authorization for bargaining demands, (K) ratification of contract terms, (L) authorization for strikes, and (M) issuance of work permits. Any change in the information required by this subsection shall be reported to the Secretary at the time the reporting labor organization files with the Secretary the annual financial report required by subsection (b) of this section.

(b) Every labor organization shall file annually with the Secretary a financial report signed by its president and treasurer or corresponding principal officers containing the following information in such detail as may be necessary accurately to disclose its financial condition and operations for its preceding fiscal year—

(1) assets and liabilities at the beginning and end of the fiscal year;

(2) receipts of any kind and the sources thereof;

(3) salary, allowances, and other direct or indirect disbursements (including reimbursed expenses) to each officer and also to each employee who, during such fiscal year, received more than $10,000 in the aggregate from such labor organization and any other labor organization affiliated with it or with which it is affiliated, or which is affiliated with the same national or international labor organization;

(4) direct and indirect loans made to any officer, employee, or member, which aggregated more than $250 during the fiscal year, together with a statement of the purpose, security, if any, and arrangements for repayment;

(5) direct and indirect loans to any business enterprise, together with a statement of the purpose,

security, if any, and arrangements for repayment; and

(6) other disbursements made by it including the purposes thereof;

all in such categories as the Secretary may prescribe.

(c) Every labor organization required to submit a report under this subchapter shall make available the information required to be contained in such report to all of its members, and every such labor organization and its officers shall be under a duty enforceable at the suit of any member of such organization in any State court of competent jurisdiction or in the district court of the United States for the district in which such labor organization maintains its principal office, to permit such member for just cause to examine any books, records, and accounts necessary to verify such report. The court in such action may, in its discretion, in addition to any judgment awarded to the plaintiff or plaintiffs, allow a reasonable attorney's fee to be paid by the defendant, and costs of the action.

209. *Penalties*

(a) Any person who willfully violates this subchapter shall be fined not more than $10,000 or imprisoned for not more than one year, or both.

(b) Any person who makes a false statement or representation of a material fact, knowing it to be false, or who knowingly fails to disclose a material fact, in any document, report, or other information required under the provisions of this subchapter shall be fined not more than $10,000 or imprisoned for not more than one year, or both.

(c) Any person who willfully makes a false entry in or willfully conceals, withholds, or destroys any books, records, reports, or statements required to be kept by any provision of this subchapter shall be fined not more than $10,000 or imprisoned for not more than one year, or both.

Title III—Trusteeships

301. *Reports*

(a) Every labor organization which has or assumes trusteeship over any subordinate labor organization shall file with the Secretary within thirty days after September 14, 1959 or the imposition of any such trusteeship, and semiannually thereafter, a report, signed by its president and treasurer or corresponding principal officers, as well as by the trustees of such subordinate labor organization, containing the following information: (1) the name and address of the subordinate organization; (2) the date of establishing the trusteeship; (3) a detailed statement of the reason or reasons for establishing or continuing the trusteeship; and (4) the nature and extent of participation by the membership of the subordinate organization in the selection of delegates to represent such organization in regular or special conventions or other policy-determining bodies and in the election of officers of the labor organization which has assumed trusteeship over such subordinate organization. The initial report shall also include a full and complete account of the financial condition of such subordinate organization as of the time trusteeship was assumed over it. During the continuance of a trusteeship the labor organization which has assumed trusteeship over a subordinate labor organization shall file on behalf of the subordinate labor organization the annual financial report required by section 210(b) of this title signed by the president and treasurer or corresponding principal officers of the labor organization which has assumed such trusteeship and the trustees of the subordinate labor organization.

(c) Any person who willfully violates this section shall be fined not more than $10,000 or imprisoned for not more than one year, or both.

(d) Any person who makes a false statement or representation of a material fact, knowing it to be false, or who knowingly fails to disclose a material fact, in any report required under the provisions of this section or willfully makes any false entry in or willfully withholds, conceals, or destroys any documents, books, records, reports, or statements upon which such report is based, shall be fined not more than $10,000 or imprisoned for not more than one year, or both.

(e) Each individual required to sign a report under this section shall be personally responsible for the filing of such report and for any statement contained therein which he knows to be false.

302. *Purposes of trusteeship*

Trusteeships shall be established and administered by a labor organization over a subordinate body only in accordance with the constitution and bylaws of the organization which has assumed trusteeship over the subordinate body and for the purpose of correcting corruption or financial malpractice, assuring the performance of collective bargaining agreements or other duties of a bargaining representative, restoring democratic procedures, or otherwise carrying out the legitimate objects of such labor organizations.

303. *Unlawful acts relating to labor organization under trusteeship*

(a) During any period when a subordinate body of a labor organization is in trusteeship, it shall be unlawful (1) to count the vote of delegates from such body in any convention or election of officers of the labor organization unless the delegates have been chosen by secret ballot in an election in which all the members in good standing of such subordinate body were eligible to participate, or (2) to transfer to such organization any current receipts or other funds of the subordinate body except the normal per capita tax and assessments payable by subordinate bodies not in trusteeship: *Provided,* That nothing herein contained shall prevent the distribution of the assets of a labor organization in accordance with its constitution and bylaws upon the bona fide dissolution thereof.

(b) Any person who willfully violates this section shall be fined not more than $10,000 or imprisoned for not more than one year, or both.

304. *Enforcement*

(a) Upon the written complaint of any member or subordinate body of a labor organization alleging that such organization has violated the provisions of this subchapter (except section 301 of this title) the Secretary shall investigate the complaint and if the Secretary finds probable cause to believe that such violation has occurred and has not been remedied he shall, without disclosing the identity of the complainant, bring a civil action in any district court of the United States having jurisdiction of the labor organization for such relief (including injunctions) as may be appropriate. Any member or subordinate body of a labor organization affected by any violation of this subchapter (except section 301 of this title) may bring a civil action in any district court of the United States having jurisdiction of the labor organization for such relief (including injunctions) as may be appropriate.

(c) In any proceeding pursuant to this section a trusteeship established by a labor organization in conformity with the procedural requirements of its constitution and bylaws and authorized or ratified after a fair hearing either before the executive board or before such other body as may be provided in accordance with its constitution or bylaws shall be presumed valid for a period of eighteen months from the date of its establishment and shall not be subject to attack during such period except upon clear and convincing proof that the trusteeship was not established or maintained in good faith for a purpose allowable under section 302 of this title. After the expiration of eighteen months the trusteeship shall be presumed invalid in any such proceeding and its discontinuance shall be decreed unless the labor organization shall show by clear and convincing proof that the continuation of the trusteeship is necessary for a purpose allowable under section 302 of this title. In the latter event the court may dismiss the complaint or retain jurisdiction of the cause on such conditions and for such period as it deems appropriate.

Title IV—Elections

401. *Terms of office and election procedures*

(a) Every national or international labor organization, except a federation of national or international labor organizations, shall elect its officers not less often than once every five years either by secret ballot among the members in good standing or at a convention of delegates chosen by secret ballot.

(b) Every local labor organization shall elect its officers not less often than once every three years by secret ballot among the members in good standing.

(c) Every national or international labor organization, except a federation of national or international labor organizations, and every local labor organization, and its officers, shall be under a duty, enforceable at the suit of any bona fide candidate for office in such labor organization in the district court of the United States in which such labor organization maintains its principal office, to comply with all reasonable requests of any candidate to distribute by mail or otherwise at the candidate's expense campaign literature in aid of such person's candidacy to all members in good standing of such labor organization and to refrain from discrimination in favor of or against any candidate with respect to the use of lists of members, and whenever such labor organizations or its officers authorize the distribution by mail or otherwise to members of campaign literature on behalf of any candidate or of the labor organization itself with reference to such election, similar distribution at the request of any other bona fide candidate shall be made by such labor organization and its officers, with equal treatment as to the expense of such distribution. Every bona fide candidate shall have the right, once within 30 days prior to an election of a labor organization in which he is a candidate, to inspect a list containing the names and last known addresses of all members of the labor organization who are subject to a collective bargaining agreement requiring membership therein as a condition of employment, which list shall be maintained and kept at the principal office of such labor organization by a designated official thereof. Adequate safeguards to insure a fair election shall be provided, including the right of any candidate to have an observer at the polls and at the counting of the ballots.

(d) Officers of intermediate bodies, such as general committees, system boards, joint boards, or joint councils, shall be elected not less often than once every four years by secret ballot among the members in good standing or by labor organization officers representative of such members who have been elected by secret ballot.

(e) In any election required by this section which is to be held by secret ballot a reasonable opportunity shall be given for the nomination of candidates and every member in good standing shall be eligible to be a candidate and to hold office (subject to section 504 of this title and to reasonable qualifications uniformly imposed) and shall have the right to vote for or otherwise support the candidate or candidates of his choice, without being subject to penalty, discipline, or improper interference or reprisal of any kind by such organization or any member thereof. Not less than fifteen days prior to the election notice thereof shall be mailed to each member at his last known home address. Each member in good standing shall be entitled to one vote. No member whose dues have been withheld by his employer for payment to such organization pursuant to his voluntary authorization provided for in a collective bargaining agreement shall be declared ineligible to vote or be a candidate for office in such organization by reason of alleged delay or default in the payment of dues. The votes cast by members of each local labor organization shall be counted, and the results published, separately. The election officials designated in the constitution and bylaws or the secretary, if no other official is designated, shall preserve for one year the ballots and all other records pertaining to the election. The election shall be conducted in accordance with the constitution and bylaws of such organization insofar as they are not inconsistent with the provisions of this subchapter.

(f) When officers are chosen by a convention of delegates elected by secret ballot, the convention shall be conducted in accordance with the constitution and bylaws of the labor organization insofar as they are not inconsistent with the provisions of this subchapter. The officials designated in the constitution and bylaws or the secretary, if no other is designated, shall preserve for one year the credentials of the delegates and all minutes and other records of the convention pertaining to the election of officers.

(g) No moneys received by any labor organization by way of dues, assessment, or similar levy, and no moneys of an employer shall be contributed or applied to promote the candidacy of any person in an election subject to the provisions of this subchapter. Such moneys of a labor organization may be utilized for notices, factual statements of issues not involving candidates, and other expenses necessary for the holding of an election.

(h) If the Secretary, upon application of any member of a local labor organization, finds after hearing in accordance with the Administrative Procedure Act that the constitution and bylaws of such labor organization do not provide an adequate procedure for the removal of an elected officer guilty of serious misconduct, such officer may be removed, for cause shown and after notice and hearing, by the members in good standing voting in a secret ballot conducted by the officers of such labor organization in accordance with its constitution and bylaws insofar as they are not inconsistent with the provisions of this subchapter.

(i) The Secretary shall promulgate rules and regulations prescribing minimum standards and procedures for determining the adequacy of the removal procedures to which reference is made in subsection (h) of this section.

402. *Enforcement*

(a) A member of a labor organization—

(1) who has exhausted the remedies available under the constitution and bylaws of such organization and of any parent body, or

(2) who has invoked such available remedies without obtaining a final decision within three calendar months after their invocation,

may file a complaint with the Secretary within one calendar month thereafter alleging the violation of any provision of section 401 of this title (including violation of the constitution and bylaws of the labor organization pertaining to the election and removal of officers). The challenged election shall be presumed valid pending a final decision thereon (as hereinafter provided) and in the interim the affairs of the organization shall be conducted by the officers elected or in such other manner as its constitution and bylaws may provide.

(b) The Secretary shall investigate such complaint and, if he finds probable cause to believe that a violation of this subchapter has occurred and has not been remedied, he shall, within sixty days after the filing of such complaint, bring a civil action against the labor organization as an entity in the district court of the United States in which such labor organization maintains its principal office to set aside the invalid election, if any, and to direct the conduct of an election or hearing and vote upon the removal of officers under the supervision of the Secretary and in accordance with the provisions of this subchapter and such rules and regulations as the Secretary may prescribe. The court shall have power to take such action as it deems proper to preserve the assets of the labor organization.

(c) If, upon a preponderance of the evidence after a trial upon the merits, the court finds—

(1) that an election has not been held within the time prescribed by section 401 of this title, or

(2) that the violation of section 401 of this title may have affected the outcome of an election,

the court shall declare the election, if any, to be void

and direct the conduct of a new election under supervision of the Secretary and, so far as lawful and practicable, in conformity with the constitution and bylaws of the labor organization. The Secretary shall promptly certify to the court the names of the persons elected, and the court shall thereupon enter a decree declaring such persons to be the officers of the labor organization. If the proceeding is for the removal of officers pursuant to subsection (h) of section 401 of this title, the Secretary shall certify the results of the vote and the court shall enter a decree declaring whether such persons have been removed as officers of the labor organization.

403

No labor organization shall be required by law to conduct elections of officers with greater frequency or in a different form or manner than is required by its own constitution or bylaws, except as otherwise provided by this subchapter. Existing rights and remedies to enforce the constitution and bylaws of a labor organization with respect to elections prior to the conduct thereof shall not be affected by the provisions of this subchapter. The remedy provided by this subchapter for challenging an election already conducted shall be exclusive.

Title V—Safeguards for labor organizations

501. *Fiduciary responsibility of officers of labor organizations*

(a) The officers, agents, shop stewards, and other representatives of a labor organization occupy positions of trust in relation to such organization and its members as a group. It is, therefore, the duty of such person, taking into account the special problems and functions of a labor organization, to hold its money and property solely for the benefit of the organization and its members and to manage, invest, and expend the same in accordance with its constitution and bylaws and any resolutions of the governing bodies adopted thereunder, to refrain from dealing with such organization as an adverse party or in behalf of an adverse party in any matter connected with his duties and from holding or acquiring any pecuniary or personal interest which conflicts with the interests of such organization, and to account to the organization for any profit received by him in whatever capacity in connection with transactions conducted by him or under his direction on behalf of the organization. A general exculpatory provision in the constitution and bylaws of such a labor organization or a general exculpatory resolution of a governing body purporting to relieve any such person of liability for breach of the duties declared by this section shall be void as against public policy.

(b) When any officer, agent, shop steward, or representative of any labor organization is alleged to have violated the duties declared in subsection (a) of this section and the labor organization or its governing board or officers refuse or fail to sue or recover damages or secure an accounting or other appropriate relief within a reasonable time after being requested to do so by any member of the labor organization, such member may sue such officer, agent, shop steward, or representative in any district court of the United States or in any State court of competent jurisdiction to recover damages or secure an accounting or other appropriate relief for the benefit of the labor organization. No such proceeding shall be brought except upon leave of the court obtained upon verified application and for good cause shown, which application may be made ex parte. The trial judge may allot a reasonable part of the recovery in any action under this subsection to pay the fees of counsel prosecuting the suit at the instance of the member of the labor organization and to compensate such member for any expenses necessarily paid or incurred by him in connection with the litigation.

(c) Any person who embezzles, steals, or unlawfully and willfully abstracts or converts to his own use, or the use of another, any of the moneys, funds, securities, property, or other assets of a labor organization of which he is an officer, or by which he is employed, directly or indirectly, shall be fined not more than $10,000 or imprisoned for not more than five years, or both.

502. *Bonding*

(a) Every officer, agent, shop steward, or other representative or employee of any labor organization (other than a labor organization whose property and annual financial receipts do not exceed $5,000 in value), or of a trust in which a labor organization is interested, who handles funds or other property thereof shall be bonded to provide protection against loss by reason of acts of fraud or dishonesty on his part directly or through connivance with others. The bond of each such person shall be fixed at the beginning of the organization's fiscal year and shall be in an amount not less than 10 per centum of the funds handled by him and his predecessor or predecessors, if any, during the preceding fiscal year, but in no case more than $500,000. . . .

504. *Prohibition against certain persons holding office; violations and penalties*

(a) No person who is or has been a member of the Communist Party or who has been convicted of, or served any part of a prison term resulting from his

conviction of, robbery, bribery, extortion, embezzle-
ment, grand larceny, burglary, arson, violation of nar-
cotics laws, murder, rape, assault with intent to kill,
assault which inflicts grievous bodily injury, or a violation of title III or IV of this chapter, or conspiracy to
commit any such crimes, shall serve—

(1) as an officer, director, trustee, member of
any executive board or similar governing body, business agent, manager, organizer, or other employee
(other than as an employee performing exclusively
clerical or custodial duties) of any labor organization, or

(2) as a labor relations consultant to a person
engaged in an industry or activity affecting com-
merce, or as an officer, director, agent, or employee
(other than as an employee performing exclusively
clerical or custodial duties) of any group or association of employers dealing with any labor organization,

during or for five years after the termination of his
membership in the Communist Party, or for five years
after such conviction or after the end of such imprison-
ment, unless prior to the end of such five-year period,
in the case of a person so convicted or imprisoned,
(A) his citizenship rights, having been revoked as a
result of such conviction, have been fully restored, or
(B) the Board of Parole of the United States Department of Justice determines that such person's service in
any capacity referred to in clause (1) or (2) would
not be contrary to the purposes of this chapter. Prior to
making any such determination the Board shall hold an
administrative hearing and shall give notice of such
proceeding by certified mail to the State, county, and
Federal prosecuting officials in the jurisdiction or juris-
dictions in which such person was convicted. The
Board's determination in any such proceeding shall be

final. No labor organization or officer thereof shall knowingly permit any person to assume or hold any office or paid position in violation of this subsection.

(b) Any person who willfully violates this section shall be fined not more than $10,000 or imprisoned for not more than one year, or both.

(c) For the purposes of this section, any person shall be deemed to have been "convicted" and under the disability of "conviction" from the date of the judgment of the trial court or the date of the final sustaining of such judgment on appeal, whichever is the later event, regardless of whether such conviction occurred before or after September 14, 1959.

503. *Making of loans; payment of fines*

(a) No labor organization shall make directly or indirectly any loan or loans to any officer or employee of such organization which results in a total indebtedness on the part of such officer or employee to the labor organization in excess of $2,000.

(b) No labor organization or employer shall directly or indirectly pay the fine of any officer or employee convicted of any willful violation of this chapter.

(c) Any person who willfully violates this section shall be fined not more than $5,000 or imprisoned for not more than one year, or both.

Title VI—Miscellaneous Provisions

601. *Investigations*

(a) The Secretary shall have power when he believes it necessary in order to determine whether any person has violated or is about to violate any provision of this chapter (except title II of this chapter) to make an investigation and in connection therewith he may enter such places and inspect such records and accounts and question such persons as he may deem necessary to enable him to determine the facts relative thereto. The Secretary may report to interested persons or officials concerning the facts required to be shown in any report required by this chapter and concerning the reasons for failure or refusal to file such a report or any other matter which he deems to be appropriate as a result of such an investigation.

APPENDIX B

The Mine Workers' Election of 1969

During the long, autocratic presidency of the late John L. Lewis, the Mine Workers Union was a major force in the coal industry. Lewis was instrumental in organizing that industry and bringing stability to its employees. After his death, Lewis was succeeded in the presidency by his hand-picked choice, W. A. (Tony) Boyle, who took office in 1962.

Boyle's leadership remained essentially unchallenged until 1969, when Joseph A. (Jock) Yablonski, a minor union officer, mounted a campaign to unseat Boyle. Boyle beat Yablonski by a substantial margin, although the election was marred by numerous violations of Title IV of the LMRDA, and was ultimately set aside. Yablonski and his wife and daughter were murdered in their home on January 1, 1970, and the tragic incident was ultimately traced to Boyle's leadership.

The Yablonski murder awakened public concern, and spurred further efforts within the union to oust the Boyle leadership. Yablonski's cudgels were taken up by Mike Trbovich, a union member, who became the formal intervening party in much of the litigation that followed. The insurgent union members formed Miners for Union Democracy, which was instrumental in galvanizing support for the challenge to Boyle and in raising outside funds for the legal struggle ahead. The major role in the litigation was undertaken by Yablonski's son, Joseph A. (Chip) Yablonski, a lawyer, and Joseph L. Rauh, Jr., a prominent Washington, D.C., lawyer who had long been active in civil-rights and civil-liberties litigation.

The massive election violations in the 1969 election were ultimately corrected, but it was not until 1972 that the litigation moved far enough along to permit a rerun election under the supervision of the Secretary of Labor. In that election Arnold Miller, who had assumed the leadership of the insurgent mine workers, defeated Boyle. Boyle, meanwhile, was involved in numerous other civil and criminal matters growing out of his misconduct while in office.

This appendix is designed to show the complex web of litigation involved in correcting abuses of Title IV and related violations of the LMRDA. The case references may help the reader to further understand the kinds of violations described in Chapter IV of this book, and to see how certain misconduct by union officers may involve several sections of the LMRDA.

The litigation costs in these cases were staggering. A substantial amount of outside funds was raised through the Miners for Union Democracy. Ultimately, the court ordered the union to pay counsel fees in much of the litigation. This litigation, which is not typical, was instrumental in awakening rank-and-file union members to the possibility of abuse by unions of the electoral process and making them aware of the machinery to correct these violations. The Yablonski-Boyle litigation also established much of the existing case law under Title IV.

We have not listed all of the cases in this appendix. Intermediate decisions and minor skirmishes on technical issues are omitted, although they too consumed much time and money. The reader may find a good factual description of the election and the violations in Hodgson v. Mine Workers Union, 344 F. Supp. 17 (D.D.C. 1972). A summary of the entire litigation may be found in Yablonski v. Mine Workers Union, 448 F.2d 1175 (D.C. Cir. 1971) *and* Yablonski v. Mine Workers Union, 466 F.2d 424 (D.C. Cir 1972).

1. A brief chronology and description of the election violations

February, 1969	Boyle aware of potential challengers for presidency.
March 1, 1969	*UMW Journal* begins to give undue coverage to incumbent UMW officers.
April 1, 1969	Union grants pay increase to officers and employees of the union, allegedly to buy their support for Boyle.
April 17, 1969	Boyle appoints Yablonski as acting director of the union's Non-Partisan League.
May 29, 1969	Yablonski announces his candidacy for the union presidency.
June 6, 1969	Boyle ousts Yablonski from his position as acting director.
June 23, 1969	Yablonski ouster formalized by union executive board.
June, 1969, and later	Various districts of Mine Workers Union use their officers and funds to support Boyle.

Summer, 1969	Funds transferred from union to locals and districts to support Boyle campaign.
Various times	Boyle campaign financed by $142,710 in contributions obtained from employees and officers of the union, on a nonvoluntary basis.
Late 1969	Union funds used for stationery and lists for Boyle mailings.
October, 1969	Union distributes pens with names of incumbent officers—pens paid for with union funds.
October, 1969, and later	Yablonski makes written demand for locations of polling places and times of polling, particularly those districts in trusteeship; receives inadequate response.
November 30, 1969	District holds rally ostensibly for black-lung campaign, but really to raise money for Boyle.
December, 1969	Pattern and practice of voting abuses: nonsecret balloting, campaigning at polling places, interference with Yablonski observers.

2. Litigation before the election

Yablonski v. Mine Workers Union, 71 LRRM 2606 (D.D.C., June 20, 1969). Preliminary injunction compelling union to distribute Yablonski's campaign literature pursuant to LMRDA Sec. 401(c).

Yablonski v. Mine Workers Union, 71 LRRM 3041 (D.D.C. July 16, 1969). Preliminary injunction restraining union from removing Yablonski from his position as acting director of union's Non-Partisan League.

Yablonski v. Mine Workers Union, 72 LRRM 2076, 72 LRRM 2172, 305 F. Supp, 868, 305 F. Supp. 876 (D.D.C. August 28, Sept. 15, Sept. 19, and Nov. 4, 1969). Various stages of injunctive relief requiring union to give equal treatment to Yablonski campaign in its *Journal*. See also Yablonski v. Mine Workers Union, 307 F. Supp. 1226 (D.D.C. Nov. 26, 1969), where court does not find union in contempt for violating previous orders.

3. Litigation after the election

Hodgson v. Mine Workers Union, 344 F. Supp. 17 (D.D.C. May 1, 1972). The principal case upholding the Secretary of Labor's findings of Title IV violations. Court finds these violations "may have affected the outcome" of the 1969 election, and orders new election, under supervision of Secretary of Labor, in December, 1972. Also requires record-keeping under Title II.

Trbovich v. Mine Workers Union, 404 U.S. 686 (Jan. 17, 1972). This case upheld the right of a member to intervene in the Secretary of Labor's Title IV action, but not to raise matters outside the scope of the Secretary's complaint against the union.

Hodgson and Trbovich, intervenor, v. Mine Workers Union, 81 LRRM 2840 (D.D.C. Nov. 15, 1972). Relates to the rerun election, particularly the right of the insurgents to use bulletin boards at places of employment, and of observers for insurgents to get time off from work.

Yablonski v. Mine Workers Union, 80 LRRM 3435

and 81 LRRM 2593 (D.D.C. August 15, 1972, and Oct. 31, 1972), Affirms that ouster of Yablonski from post of acting director violates LMRDA Sec. 609. Awards no compensatory damages to Yablonski's estate, but awards punitive damages against Boyle of $3,000.

Yablonski v. Mine Workers Union, 466 F.2d 424 (D.C. Cir. Aug. 3, 1972). Awards counsel fees to Yablonski's attorneys in the litigation involving the election.

4. Related litigation

Yablonski v. Mine Workers Union, 448 F.2d 1175 (D.C. Cir. July 21, 1971) and 454 F.2d 1036 (D.C. Cir. Nov. 24, 1971). Section 501 suit against union officers for breach of their fiduciary obligations and for accounting and restoration of misappropriated funds. Court disqualifies both outside counsel and regular house counsel from defending union in this suit because those lawyars had been involved in defense of Boyle in other litigation and lacked objectivity to properly defend this suit.

Blankenship v. Boyle, 329 F. Supp. 1089 and 337 F. Supp. 296 (D.D.C. April 28, 1971, and Jan. 7, 1972). Action by pensioners against trustees of pension fund. Court finds trustees abused their position of trust. Orders ouster of Boyle and others as trustees. Latter case awards counsel fees.

Hodgson v. Mine Workers Union, 80 LRRM 2471 (D.D.C. May 24, 1972). Actions under Title III of LMRDA. Declares trusteeships, imposed by union over most of the union's twenty-three districts, to be improper trusteeships under Title III.